project dad

project dad

The Complete Do-It-Yourself Guide
for Becoming a Great Father

Todd Cartmell

Revell

a division of Baker Publishing Group
Grand Rapids, Michigan

© 2011 by Todd Cartmell

Published by Revell
a division of Baker Publishing Group
P.O. Box 6287, Grand Rapids, MI 49516-6287
www.revellbooks.com

Printed in the United States of America

All rights reserved. No part of this publication may be reproduced, stored in a retrieval system, or transmitted in any form or by any means—for example, electronic, photocopy, recording—without the prior written permission of the publisher. The only exception is brief quotations in printed reviews.

Library of Congress Cataloging-in-Publication Data
Cartmell, Todd, 1962–
    Project dad : the complete do-it-yourself guide for becoming a great father /
Todd Cartmell.
       p.   cm.
    Includes bibliographical references (p.   ).
    ISBN 978-0-8007-1999-9 (pbk.)
    1. Fathers—Religious life. 2. Fatherhood—Religious aspects—Christianity.
I. Title.
    BV4529.17.C36 2011
    248.8′421—dc22
                                          2010045880

Unless otherwise indicated, Scripture quotations are taken from the Holy Bible, New International Version®, NIV®. Copyright © 1973, 1978, 1984 by Biblica, Inc.™ Used by permission of Zondervan. All rights reserved worldwide. www.zondervan.com

Scripture marked NLT is taken from the *Holy Bible*, New Living Translation, copyright © 1996. Used by permission of Tyndale House Publishers, Inc., Wheaton, Illinois 60189. All rights reserved.

DISCLAIMER: The names and details of the children, families, and situations described in this book have been carefully changed or presented in composite form, in order to provide the reader with examples of actual experiences while ensuring the privacy of the many wonderful children, teens, and parents the author has been privileged to work with.

11   12   13   14   15   16   17   7   6   5   4   3   2   1

In keeping with biblical principles of creation stewardship, Baker Publishing Group advocates the responsible use of our natural resources. As a member of the Green Press Initiative, our company uses recycled paper when possible. The text paper of this book is comprised of 30% postconsumer waste.

This book is dedicated to my wife,
Lora, and my two sons, Jake and Luke,
of whom I am so proud and
who have been instrumental in
my becoming a father in the first place.
And a special dedication to my dad,
who has given me the best "living picture"
that any son could hope for.

Contents

7

Contents

Acknowledgments

I am indebted to many people involved in the writing of this book. I am ever so grateful to my editors, Vicki Crumpton and Wendy Wetzel, for being a pleasure to work with and for letting me know when my jokes were too "locker room." The Revell team was outstanding, and I'd like to give special thanks to Janelle Mahlmann, Cheryl Van Andel, and Melanie Evans, who worked tirelessly on this project (between breaks, of course). I'd also like to thank my friends Joe Petit, Eric Rojas, and Paul Sather (all great dads) for their helpful feedback on a few chapters and especially for their advice for me to not quit my day job.

/ / / / / / / CAUTION / / / / / / / /

You are about to begin your own Project Dad.
Your kids and family will never be the same.
Proceed at your own risk!

Introduction

The Opportunity of a Lifetime

You and I already have one thing in common. We are both dads. As dads, we've had our good moments, such as learning how to change a diaper and watch ESPN's *SportsCenter* at the same time. However, we've had a few bonehead moments along the way as well. If you have any doubt about this, just check with your wife.

But that is not our most important similarity. Despite our God-given aversion to asking for directions, you and I both have a different kind of GPS set deep in the center of our hearts. Behind all the mental clutter created by work, coaching kindergarten soccer, and pretending to know the cause of the strange noise in our car engine ("Honey, *everyone* knows what that noise means . . ."*), there is an ever-present, heat-seeking, God-instilled desire.

We want to be great dads.

*You have no idea what that noise means.

If I have to run an errand, I try to take one or both of my boys with me if I can, just so we can be together. When they were younger they considered this great fun, and of course, there was always the possibility of scoring a chocolate doughnut as well. One Saturday morning, as we were headed out on our errand, three-year-old Luke looked at me with a beaming smile and said, "Dad, you're the best." *Y'know, he's got a point there*, I thought to myself. However, just as I was getting ready to double his daily allowance of Goldfish crackers, five-year-old Jake chimed in with a correction to what he obviously perceived to be the erroneous statement previously made by his younger brother and said, "Well, he's not the *very, very, very, very* best, but he's pretty good." To my dismay, Luke quickly reversed his position and agreed with his older brother. There was no increase in Goldfish that day.

Twelve years and countless therapy hours later,* my boys have become young men. Tonight, one of them is driving— yes, I said driving—to a high school "lockdown" at a friend's church, and the other is playing in a local basketball tournament. I haven't had the guts to ask them if they think I'm a great dad. I'm not even sure if I should. I'm afraid they'd both answer, "*You're a dad?*" Either way, I suspect that their answer might be influenced by the fact that I control their access to video games.

Here is a survey form I was thinking about having them fill out:

Survey
(check the appropriate boxes)
1. My dad is a great dad. ☐ Yes ☐ No
2. I want to play video games again at some point in the future. ☐ Yes ☐ No
Name: _____
Date: _____

*The therapy was for me, of course.

All joking aside, I am fortunate to have a great relationship with my boys. They are wonderful young men who have filled my life with enough joy and laughter for a hundred lifetimes. If I were to die today, I would consider myself to have had the best experience as a father anyone could ever have.*

However, I have never met your kids. I don't know their strengths and weaknesses, their temperaments, their likes and dislikes, their hobbies and achievements, or for some, their particular areas of challenge. I don't know if they are easygoing or strong-willed, athletic or electronically inclined. But I do know one thing: in the way that is right for them, God made them to be great. Totally, 100 percent great. I hope someone in the next room heard you say a rousing "amen" to that. And if you want to raise great kids, the first step is to become a great dad.

A Few Dad Facts

One day a little girl asked her mother, "Is it true that Santa Claus brings us our Christmas presents?"

"Yes."

"And does the stork bring us babies?"

"Yes."

"And the police department protects us?"

"Yes."

"Then what do we need daddy for?"[1]

I could rattle off a bunch of statistics about the difference that dads make in their kids' lives. The thing is, you don't need me to do that. You know in your heart that your kids need a great dad. God placed that knowledge in you the second you first laid eyes on that little scrunched-up face peeking out at you through their blue or pink hospital blanket. Your kids were made by a great God to be great kids. No argument there. So where do you come in to the equation? Simple. Those kids are counting on you to be a great dad.

---

*Except for the dying part.

But just in case you're the type that likes facts, here are a few you might find interesting:

- Boys whose fathers offered praise and compliments performed better on tests of cognitive achievement than boys whose fathers were cool and aloof.
- Harsh and inconsistent discipline by fathers had a negative effect on their sons' emotional adjustment and classroom behavior, which was related to lower academic achievement.
- Higher levels of father involvement in activities with their children, such as eating meals together and helping with homework, are associated with fewer behavior problems, higher levels of sociability, and a high level of school performance among children and adolescents.
- When both fathers and mothers are involved in children's schooling, there is a higher likelihood that children will get high grades and enjoy school.[2]
- Fathers who urinate standing up have a greater proportion of children who become either life insurance salesmen or firefighters.*

This should confirm what you already know. Every kid needs a great dad. Unfortunately, not every kid gets one. Our job is to make sure that your kid does.

Spandex Not Required

In case you're stuck on some stereotype of what a great dad might look like, I've got some good news for you: great dads come in all shapes and sizes. You don't have to be a former NFL quarterback or be able to build a sports car from scratch to be a great dad. When I helped my son Jake make his Pinewood Derby car for Cub Scouts, his car came in dead last.

*I made this one up. Just wanted to make sure you're still awake.

It wasn't even tied for last place. A car with square wheels might even have come in faster.

As chief engineer on that project, I couldn't help but feel a little responsibility for our dismal last-place performance. As Jake and I went to pick up his car from the racetrack, I wondered if any of the do-it-yourself, I-built-a-house-yester-day-what-did-you-do? fathers were secretly watching to see which dad was responsible for the last-place car so they could smugly smirk at my obvious aerodynamic incompetence. I think my fake nose and mustache did the trick.

The point of this pitiful racing story is that my success as a dad is not tied to my success as a Pinewood Derby car builder. And neither is yours. You can know nothing about Pinewood Derby cars and still be a great dad. Listen to the words of Dixie Wilson, from Tim Russert's *Wisdom of Our Fathers*, as she describes her ordinary but great dad:

> My dad taught me to tie my shoes, to cross the street, to get an education, and to believe in my country, my God, and my family. I never had to look far for my hero. He was just across the living room, sitting in his favorite chair, reading the newspaper and watching the nightly news.[3]

Encouraging words for everyday, not-particularly-talented guys like me. I don't imagine that Dixie's dad was a superhero who walked around in tight, blue spandex pants. At least she never mentioned that. But he had a great impact on his daughter nonetheless. When it gets right down to it, every one of us has the ability to be a great dad. It's part of who God designed us to be.

Project Dad

In my work as a psychologist, I spend a lot of time teaching people how to take control of what they think. With that in mind, here's a key thought I'd like to drop into your brain:

God made me to be a great dad. Read this key thought out loud to yourself. Let it reverberate through your mind until its truth penetrates the very core of your being. God did not make you to be a mediocre dad. He did not sit down on his throne at the beginning of creation, cross his legs, and say to himself, "I need at least one mediocre dad. How about _____ (insert your name here)?" He made you to be a great dad. Nothing less.

In some ways, building a great dad is similar to building a Pinewood Derby car. When Jake and I were building his Pinewood Derby car, we started with a block of wood. When building a dad, God starts with a man, whom most women consider to have the emotional sensitivity of a block of wood. But that's where the similarities end. When God builds a dad, you become much more than just a lifeless block of wood. You are a *living* block of wood. You breathe, you move, you think.* In fact, God has determined that he will *not* build a great dad without your active participation. This means that you are both the *end result* of the project and an *integral participant* in the building process at the same time. Jesus said, "I stand at the door and knock" (Rev. 3:20). It is up to us to open the door and allow him in to let the building process begin. God is the foreman of the project with all the resources in the universe. However, this is one project he will not complete without you.

The Five Key Areas

Let's review the main point so far: God is building a dad, and that dad is you. And God's plan is for you to be a great dad for the kids he has entrusted into your care. Five key areas are essential for becoming the great dad God wants you to be and that your children need you to be. To help you remember each area, I've connected each one with a body part, because

*At least you breathe and move. Well, at least you breathe.

as my wife keeps reminding me, guys think with their body parts. Here they are from top to bottom:

- Your eyes—how you *look* at your children
- Your mouth—how you *talk* to your children
- Your heart—how you *connect* with your children
- Your hands—how you *act* toward your children
- Your feet—how you *lead* your children

In the following pages, you will learn how to:

- *look* at your children in a way that will help them see the reflection of who God made them to be in your eyes;
- *talk* to your children in a way that will nurture them and shape how they learn to think about themselves;
- *connect* with your children in a way that will build a relationship that will stay strong for years to come;
- *act* toward your children in a way that will open them up to the lessons and wisdom they need to learn from you; and
- *lead* your children along the path that God has laid out for them and protect them from the pitfalls and traps the enemy has laid ahead of them.

Becoming a Great Dad

I remember standing beside Lora at Huntington Memorial Hospital in Pasadena, California, preparing to give birth to our first son. Actually, Lora was the one who was preparing to give birth; I was looking for something solid to lean on. My life (not to mention my appreciation for the elasticity of the female anatomy) was forever changed that day as I saw Jake enter this world. I remember holding him, tightly wrapped in his hospital blankets, for the first time. His small, blue-tinted body and the little blue hat the nurse put on him made him look like a Smurf. My life changed all over again the day Luke joined our family, two years later.

My guess is that your life also changed the minute you became a dad. You stepped into a whole new dimension of purpose and meaning that was more than anything you had imagined. You looked into your little baby's eyes and saw a new little person, utterly dependent upon you, whose life was now inextricably connected to yours and whose future was waiting to be written.

That little boy or girl needs a great dad.

In many ways, I am writing this book for me as much as for you. I also want to be a great dad for my two boys. However, as I write each section, I am reminded of the times I have not been a perfect dad—times when I have let my frustration get the better of me, when I have allowed my eyes to lustfully wander instead of setting an example of purity and obedience, or when I have allowed too much time to pass between family times or one-on-one check-ins with my boys. Remember, this book is about how to become a great dad—becoming a perfect dad is above my pay grade.

Being a great dad means being an authentic dad. It means being a dad who:

- is willing to recognize his sins and shortcomings and humbly ask God (and others, if necessary) to forgive him;
- will ask God to shape him into the man God wants him to be; and
- is willing to do whatever is necessary to become that man.

I really don't think it was by accident that God spoke to Balaam through a donkey (you can read the play-by-play in Numbers 22). He could have chosen an armadillo or a centipede for that matter. No, I suspect that God knew that there

18

would be many dads through the centuries who, like myself, would need a visual reminder that he can work through them even if they occasionally act like the target of a pin the tail on the donkey game.

At the end of each chapter, I have included a list of key points and discussion questions to help you put the ideas from each chapter to work. I encourage you to use every idea in this book to make the impact on your children that only you can make. The truth is that time is already ticking on your Project Dad; now it is just a question of what kind of dad you and God are going to build.

Your kids are hoping that you build a great dad. Nine out of ten dentists recommend the same.

Key Points

1. Every child needs a great dad.
2. Luckily for your kids, God designed *you* to be a great dad.
3. In order to help you become a great dad, God needs your active participation.
4. There are five key areas that every dad needs to work on to be a great dad.
5. A great dad is not a perfect dad but an authentic dad.

Getting to Work

1. Why do you think a father has such an important impact on his kids?
2. Read Philippians 1:6 and 4:13. Name one victory and one failure you've had as a dad. How does Paul's encouragement to us apply to the ups and downs of being a dad?
3. List three characteristics you want God to build *into you* as a dad by completing this sentence: "I want to be a dad who . . ."

4. List two characteristics you want God to build *out of you* as a dad by completing this sentence: "I want to be a dad who doesn't . . ."
5. Identify one action step you will take to build a positive dad characteristic and one action step to eliminate a negative dad characteristic. Choose a close friend and tell that person what those action steps are. Ask that person to check with you in a week to see how you are doing.

PART 1

How You Look at Your Children

Who Are These Little People?

(And Why Are They in My House?)

I'd like to introduce you to my two sons. Jake is my oldest. As I write this, I can't believe that he is sixteen years old and almost done with high school. He loves to have fun—anytime, anywhere, and with anyone. Just as I tend to be a little on the introverted side, Jake is a little on the extroverted side. Did I say a little? Scratch that. He loves meeting new people and will start up a conversation with anyone who will listen. In fact, when he runs out of listeners, he just starts talking to himself in the bathroom mirror (you think I'm joking).

On a more testosterone-enhanced note, Jake has earned his black belt in Shotokan karate and has been a national champion for his age and belt rank. I remember being moved with tears of joy the day he first kicked someone in the head. (Now that's something you don't usually hear a mother say.)

I can see Jake's love for God and Christian faith growing by leaps and bounds as he really tries to be a good representative for God at school and with his friends. Jake has shown maturity beyond his years in his choice of friends and has a wonderful group of awesome friends who are great kids and, as far as I know, have no police records.

My youngest son, Luke, is naturally quick-witted. I take personal responsibility for introducing him to the concept of the practical joke, a mistake I am still paying for today. Luke is the reason that when we had a landline phone in our house (remember those?), all four phones would simultaneously play different ringtones when someone called. It sounded like a circus gone bad. Like his brother, Luke brings lots of laughter into our family. He and Jake get along better than any set of brothers I have ever seen, and it brings a deep feeling of delight to my heart to hear them laughing away as they brush their teeth and pop their zits each night before bed.

Luke decided to retire from his short career of playing saxophone in the school band in favor of joining the football and basketball teams. Since he is currently in middle school, we have already had multiple experiences with anonymous girls calling our house (obviously from an unsupervised pajama party), asking for Luke, and then telling him, between giggles, that they are calling on behalf of a different girl, whom he has never heard of. Luke is also developing a great group of friends and often prays for them at bedtime, asking God for opportunities to be a good example and to share his faith.

Different Shades of Great

The goal of this chapter is to get you thinking about what makes each of your kids special. This means paying attention to detail. Your wife may not think that you, as a dad, pay much attention to the important details of life, such as the color of paint in your family room. You, however, are satisfied with the general notion that there probably *is* paint in your family room and choose to spend the rest of your mental energy focusing on details that are much more vital to your survival, such as whether there are any BBQ chips left in the pantry.

Perhaps an example from the animal kingdom would help. If you had a couple of penguins for children, I, as a casual observer, would not be able to tell them apart. (Of course, if you had penguins for children, you would have bigger problems than can be addressed in this book.) You, however, as the alpha father penguin, would be able to easily tell them apart. You would know the subtle differences in the lines of their coloring. You would hear the different intonations in their little penguin voices. You would know that your penguin boy prefers his fish raw while your penguin girl likes her fish lightly grilled, with a touch of Grey Poupon on the side.

Luckily, God has made it a little easier for us dads than that. In his book *What a Difference a Daddy Makes*, psychologist Kevin Leman tells the story of how he used to bring his kids a bakery treat on Fridays. My question would be, *why limit the bakery trips to just Fridays?* but I digress. Instead of just getting half a dozen doughnuts or a standard variety pack, Leman would take the extra time to pick out the special type of doughnut that each of his children liked the best. Listen to the detail:

> Holly and Kevin both wanted chocolate éclairs, all the time. Hannah liked a little more variety. Sometimes I'd get her an éclair and sometimes I'd get her a doughnut. Lauren had to have a doughnut *with sprinkles*. She liked to lick off the sprinkles and frosting and then throw away the rest. Since she never ate the cake part, she wouldn't know what to do with an éclair. Krissy liked these dainty little cakes called *petits fours*.[1]

Here's the message Leman was communicating to his children: "There are five of you, but I know each one of you very well. I don't take you for granted. I never forget that you are individuals. You matter to me."[2] Leman's kids were each a different shade of great, and he knew it. What a difference a doughnut makes.

The Difference Is in the Details

Your kids' individual differences and special qualities are not that difficult to spot, once you take the time to look for them. Here is a list of questions that will help you identify some of the things that make each of your kids special and unique. Test yourself to see if you can answer all questions for each child (and yes, it is cheating to ask your wife).

Things That Are Special about My Child

1. What is my child's favorite movie?
2. What does my child love to do in his/her free time?
3. What is my child's favorite sport or organized activity?
4. What is my child's favorite book?
5. How would my child describe God?
6. How does my child like to relax?
7. Does my child's tank get filled up by spending time with friends, with family, or alone?
8. What is one trait my child has picked up from his/her mother?
9. What is one trait my child has picked up from his/her father?
10. Where would my child like to go on a dream vacation?
11. What is one of my child's biggest weaknesses or challenges?
12. What is an important life lesson my child needs to learn?
13. What is one of my child's biggest strengths?
14. Who is my child's closest friend?
15. What is my child's favorite restaurant?
16. How does my child handle disappointment?
17. How well does my child deal with frustration and anger?

18. What does my child worry about?
19. What is a good habit that my child needs to develop?
20. Is my child becoming a good problem-solver?
21. How well does my child get along with kids his/her own age?
22. What does my child pray about?
23. What is something my child wants to improve at?
24. What does my child like about him/herself?
25. How does my child make our family special?

Scoring chart:

25 correct: I said it was cheating to ask your wife.

20–24 correct: Nice job. You are on your way to becoming a great dad.

15–19 correct: Average job. You are on your way to being on your way to becoming a great dad.

14 or less: Yes, those are *your* children. Introduce yourself at your earliest convenience.

One of the nice things about these twenty-five questions is that the answers to them are always changing because your children are always changing. You might find it helpful to revisit these questions now and then to make sure you are staying in tune with the special children God has given you. In fact, you could hit a home run by sitting down with each of your children individually and discussing these questions together to see if your answers match up.

Blue and Pink Sprinkles

It never really mattered to me whether Lora and I had boys or girls, as I figured it would be fun either way. As it turns out, we have two wonderful boys. However, in my work as a child psychologist, I have had the opportunity to get to know hundreds of delightful girls of every age who came to see me because of problems with anxiety, anger control, and everything in between.

Because there's no getting around the fact that girls and boys are different species, I will use both boy and girl examples throughout this book. But I have to tell you that in addition to the differences between the species,* I have seen plenty of variation *within* each species. For example, I've seen naturally athletic boys who thrive on sports, and I've seen boys who take a pass on sports in favor of other areas, such as electronics or music. I've seen girls who are dainty and soft-spoken as well as rough-and-tumble girls who can scream the paint off the side of a barn.

But despite their gender and individual personality differences, I have noticed that every boy and girl I have ever met have a few important things in common. They *all* want to feel loved and accepted. They *all* want to know that they are valuable and important. And they *all* need a great dad who takes the time to know what kind of penguin they are.

Know Your Clubs, I Mean, Your Kids

When you take the time to think about the things that make each of your children special and unique, it shows your children how important they are to you. I know some dads who could easily tell me the slightest difference between each of their golf clubs in great detail. The different sizes, shapes, scratches, and accomplishments that make each club unique. The club that hit the hole in one. The club that made that awesome chip shot last spring.

But how many of those clubs can trigger a waterfall of wonderful memories and make you whisper a prayer of thanksgiving to God for putting them in your life? Okay,

*Girls use paint to express themselves by painting pictures of houses, flowers, and cute animals that they will cherish forever. Boys shoot paint at each other with semiautomatic weapons that will leave golf-ball-sized welts that they will cherish forever.

bad example. Let me try again. How many of those clubs will unleash fountains of tears the day they gather up their belongings and move off to college?

Not too long ago, I was talking with my friend Mark, whose oldest son, Louis, just left for college in Indiana. Mark is a good friend who has coached baseball and basketball for all three of his sons for years. His youngest son Michael and my son Luke also became good friends, and Mark is the assistant coach on their travel basketball team. After basketball practice one afternoon, while the kids were putting their gear in their bags, I asked Mark how he was handling Louis's departure.

"I'm a real weenie about this stuff, man," he told me, looking at me with sadness in his eyes. "It's really hard to see him go. I just can't help but cry. I can't stop it. Man, this is a lot harder than I thought it was going to be." Some of you might think that Mark should lose a "Man Card" for such drivel. On the contrary, I think he earned one. Something tells me that Mark's kids know that they are way more important to their dad than his golf clubs.

In his book *Fatherhood*, Bill Cosby jokes that when his father was angry at him, he would dryly say, "I brought you into this world and I can take you out. It don't make no difference to me. I'll just make another one like you."[3] The humor in those words is that we all know how untrue they are. There will never be another boy or girl like _____ (insert your child's name). Your child is handmade by God, priceless, and designed to last forever. Not even Arnold Palmer can say that about his golf clubs.

Recognizing the things that make each of your children special is step one toward becoming a great dad. As you become more aware of their unique qualities and the important details of their lives, you will be better able to fine-tune your fathering approach to most effectively guide your children in the areas they need your help with the most. Just as a mountaineer studies every detail of the mountain he is going to

29

climb in order to find the best way to the summit, knowing the special details that make each of your children unique will help you find the right path to their hearts.

Key Points

1. God made each of your children special and unique.
2. Many of their unique characteristics will change over time.
3. As dads, we *can* pay attention to details (such as Babe Ruth's lifetime batting average), and we need to pay attention to details about our kids.
4. Staying in touch with the details of our kids' lives makes them feel valuable and loved.
5. When you are aware of your kids' uniqueness, you will be better equipped to father them the right way.

Getting to Work

1. Name one or two friends who know you *really* well. How does it help you to have someone know your victories and struggles, your strengths and weaknesses, and still like and love you?
2. Read Psalm 139:13–16. With this passage in mind, identify two traits about each of your kids that make them a unique and awesome person.
3. Sit down with each of your kids and talk through the twenty-five questions. Did you feel more connected when you were done? How did your child respond? How do you think it made your child feel to know that you are really interested in his/her life?
4. Based on your child's answers to the twenty-five questions, identify one area each of your kids needs your help with. Now identify one practical way that you will help.
5. How will your prayer time be impacted by what you learned from the twenty-five questions?

There's a Prize Inside

How do you spell adventure? As a seven-year-old Canadian boy who didn't get out much in the frozen tundra, I spelled it, "looking for the prize in the specially marked cereal box." The only thing more exciting was calling local residents and asking them if their refrigerator was running—and if so, advising them to go catch it.

My first step in this weekly adventure would be to carefully read the description on the side of the box to identify the little toy or gadget that I was looking for as I began my search-and-rescue mission. Once I had opened the box, the battle would begin, namely getting through the airtight, waterproof, machine-gun-resistant plastic bag they put the cereal in. I could never figure out why they make those bags so hard to open. After all, you are supposed to *eat* the cereal, aren't you?

I remember pulling on that bag with all the strength my little fingers could muster. Eventually my fingers would slip off, and the bag would just laugh at me in mock triumph. I would try again and again, with no visible sign that I had even bothered the bag at all. I knew God said not to hate anybody, but I couldn't help it. I hated that bag. It was at that point that I would bring in the reserves, canines included. With one swift motion, I ripped into the bag with every tooth that was still in working condition (I played hockey, eh), like a bulldog attacking a tasty new chew toy. I pulled, bit, and tugged with unbridled fury, the cheers of the crowd in my ears, the dust of the coliseum floor burning my eyes, the glory of the arena pumping through my veins.

Okay, that's enough melodrama for a men's book. The point is that I finally broke through the security-enforced bag and peered into the cereal, hoping the prize might have shifted toward the top of the box. Typically, it hadn't. So I had to plunge my unwashed hands* into the depths of the cereal, stretching my fingers to feel the paper wrapping that housed my prize.

When I finally retrieved the prize I had so valiantly fought for, it was worth every ounce of sweat that I had dripped into the cereal. If the prize was a tattoo, I wore that tattoo with pride until it faded from sight. If it was a little toy gadget, it immediately became my favorite possession (until it broke, thirty seconds later). The fight was over, and I was the victor. There had been a prize inside the box, hidden where no one could see, and I had found it.

Open the Box

The reason I share this uneventful example from my even more uneventful childhood is that I think fathering is very similar to my childhood quest for the cereal box prize. Each of your children is like an unopened cereal box. And each child has several special prizes inside, placed there by the

*I had just finished cleaning the hamster cage.

Manufacturer himself. The only difference is that with cereal, you know what prize you're looking for. With children, you have to discover them.

Have you ever wondered what prizes, what special gifts and talents, God has placed in each of your children? I wonder that all the time. First Peter 4:10 reminds us that God has given all of us certain gifts and abilities: "Each one should use whatever gift he has received to serve others, faithfully administering God's grace in its various forms." I'm always looking for little hints or glimpses of a special ability, an area of passion, or a personality trait that could grow into something special for each of my boys.

For example, just the other day, Jake had a chance to give his first private karate lesson to a young student. When I got home from work that night, Lora proudly told me what a great job Jake had done in his teaching debut. He had carefully planned out the drills and skills he wanted to focus on during the lesson, placing them in strategic order and allotting a certain amount of time for each. He had also made a list for his little student of many specific things to do at home, such as pruning his own bonsai tree and catching a fly with chopsticks. Whether Jake knows it or not, there may be a little Mr. Miyagi inside of him, just waiting to be discovered.

The Prize Might Surprise You

My mother made me take organ lessons when I was six years old, and I really didn't like it very much. The only organ playing I had ever heard was from the old guy who played the organ at the local movie theater in Powell River, British Columbia, before the movie and during the intermission. As a young kid, I thought he was kind of scary, and I was afraid my parents might be grooming me to someday take his place. Luckily, I was able to persuade my parents to let me quit organ lessons before my entire young Canadian social life was ruined, and I quickly joined the nearest hockey team I could find.

Who would have known that eight years later I would take up jazz piano (no, my mom didn't make me), decide to be a professional musician, and end up playing jazz piano gigs all over Orange County during my college years. I even wrote a tune that got airplay on "smooth jazz" stations across the country. No one saw that coming from a curly-haired hockey player with glasses and acne, I can assure you.

Here's another one that no one saw coming. In his book *100 Ways to Motivate Yourself*, author Steve Chandler tells about the time he was a reporter for the *Tucson Citizen*. One of his assignments was to interview a relatively new actor. This actor happened to be the world champion bodybuilder Arnold Schwarzenegger. At the time Arnold was promoting his third movie, *Stay Hungry*. (I think five people saw that movie.)

During the interview, Chandler asked Arnold what his future plans were. Arnold looked him square in the eye and replied, "I'm going to be the number one box-office star in all of Hollywood." Chandler writes that he had to consciously conceal his shock at this outrageous comment. Here was a huge, muscle-bound man with biceps the size of St. Louis (he won six consecutive Mr. Olympia titles), an Austrian accent so thick you could serve it alongside smoked vienna sausage, and acting chops that made Benji look like an Oscar nominee. Yet he was absolutely convinced that he could become a major motion picture star.

His curiosity aroused, Chandler asked Arnold just how he planned to accomplish this feat. "It's the same process I used in bodybuilding," Arnold replied with a straight face. "What you do is create a vision of who you want to be, and then live into that picture as if it were already true."[1]

Unless you've been hiding under a rock for the past twenty years (for some guys I know, that is a distinct possibility), you already know the rest of the story. Following that conversation, Arnold did go on to become the largest box-office draw in Hollywood for many years. His hit movies include some of your classic favorites, such as the Terminator series, *Predator*, and *Commando*, to name a few. Oh, and did I mention he also became the governor of California? Twice.

Deep inside those layers of muscle were gifts and abilities that nobody knew were there. Except for God. He's the one who put them there. And he has planted a special arrangement of gifts, abilities, and traits in your child that he designed to bloom forth like a beautiful bouquet of flowers to his glory. And he'd like you to help your child discover them.

And the Prize Is . . .

As you are looking for the special gifts and talents that God has planted in your child, here are three areas you want to be watching for:

1. *Special abilities.* These are often the easiest to spot. They are the things that your child is just naturally good at. I wasn't "naturally" good at *anything* until my piano-playing gene kicked in when I was fourteen, so have patience if you don't see anything just yet. In fact, if you're like a lot of dads, you are still waiting for *your* very first area of special ability to emerge. Don't give up—who knows, you may have a monster skill at shuffleboard just waiting to be unleashed.

Areas of special ability to watch for are too numerous for me to list completely but might include some of the following:

Reading	Drawing	Creative writing
Football	Bowling	Swimming
Dance	Baseball	Basketball
Storytelling	Computers	Math
Teaching	Humor	Martial arts
Singing	Playing an instrument	Intellectual ability
Drama	Electronics	Video games
Mechanical ability	Gymnastics	Debate/persuasion
Magic tricks	Languages	Cooking
Interior design	Art	Chess

2. *Special passions.* Areas of passion are interests or activities that your child just loves to do. When I was in my late teens, I told my parents, "I want to be a professional musician."* For some reason, however, they didn't panic. Perhaps it was because they heard me practicing six to eight hours every day. I never once heard them complain about the endless hours of scales they endured as I banged away on our upright piano in the living room of our single-story, three-bedroom house. In fact, they encouraged me every step of the way. For that time in my life, playing the piano was my passion.

I know many kids who don't have a passion—yet. If your child hasn't developed a real area of passion yet, don't sweat it. Trust the timing to God. Your job is to create an atmosphere where passions have a chance to develop. Encourage your kids to try new things, such as cleaning up their room. If a certain area isn't their cup of tea, allow them to switch course within a reasonable time frame and try something else. The main thing is that they keep dusting away until they uncover some of the jewels God has hidden within them.

3. *Special personality traits.* The thing that separates us from a piece of cardboard is our personality. I'll admit, for some it's a close call. But each of us has a whole set of special personality traits. Personality theorists believe that personality traits are the product of both our genetics and our environment. This means that while we are born with certain personality tendencies, they are shaped by our experiences over time.

In other words, nothing is set in stone. Think about some of the personality traits that you see in your children. Even if your child is "a chip off the old block," don't assume that he or she will be like you in every way. Each of our boys has traits that come from both Lora and myself.† Here is a list of

*Code for "I am going to deliver pizza for the rest of my life."
†Social grace from her, drooling from me.

positive personality traits. Identify the ones you see emerging in each of your children:

Leader	Humorous	Faithful
Outgoing	Considerate	Compassionate
Witty	Reflective	Confident
Caring	Hard working	Strong
Honest	Cheerful	Easygoing
Focused	Responsible	Teachable
Brave	Creative	Self-motivated
Persistent	Positive outlook	Encouraging

Every Box Has a Prize

By now you should be able to identify some of the special abilities, passions, and personality traits God has placed inside your kids. As you keep watching, you will find that these gifts will continue to evolve and new ones will emerge over time as well.

Perhaps your child is talented at art, has a passion for sports, or is naturally humorous and encouraging to others. Whatever your child's special areas are, let her know that you have noticed these strengths, or gifts, that God has given her. ("Hey sweetie, you have a really great sense of humor, but I don't think that wearing a clown nose to school is going to work.") For some ability areas, such as playing an instrument, establishing a reasonable practice schedule to nurture an ability is appropriate. The goal is to help your children find areas of enjoyment, competence, and success that will contribute to their overall sense of confidence and self-esteem and to understand that these gifts have been placed in their cereal box from God.

Nothing is sadder to a young Canadian boy than never discovering the prize inside the cereal box. Unfortunately, many children have never had a father to help them find and nurture their own special gifts. The result is that some of their gifts will remain dormant, hidden like buried treasure that has never been uncovered.

The fact is that God has placed many "prizes" inside your child. The question is whether you will help your child discover them. If you are a dad who is on the lookout for them, then you will experience the thrill of seeing the look of joy on your child's face as she uncovers yet another of the many special abilities, passions, and traits God has given her. Decide today to be a dad who will help your child discover for herself what God has said about her all along: that she truly is "fearfully and wonderfully made" (Ps. 139:14).

Key Points

1. God has placed many special prizes inside your child.
2. You may find a few talents and abilities that you didn't expect.
3. Your child's special abilities, passions, and personality traits will develop and evolve over time.
4. *Every* child has many prizes in their box.
5. Your job is to create a positive and encouraging atmosphere that will allow your child to discover the gifts God has placed in him or her.

Getting to Work

1. What is an area of strength or giftedness that you have? Did someone encourage you in that area? What impact did that encouragement have on you?
2. Name one special ability or talent that each of your children have. How can you encourage them in developing that ability?
3. Name one area of passion you see growing in each of your children. Letting your imagination run wild—how do you think God might use that area for his glory?

4. List one positive personality trait that you see developing in each of your children. How can you nurture that trait?
5. Read Ephesians 2:10; Colossians 3:17; and 1 Peter 4:10. What are some ways that you can encourage your children to honor and serve God with the abilities, passions, and traits that he has given them?

What Are You Looking For?

In the movie *Meet the Parents*, Ben Stiller portrays Greg (real name: Gaylord) Focker, the likable but bumbling boyfriend, who comes under the suspicious eye of his girlfriend's ex-CIA father, Jack Byrnes, played by Robert De Niro. The movie centers on the weekend that Greg and his girlfriend, Pam, spend at her parents' house for her sister's wedding. Behind the scenes, Greg is secretly planning to propose to Pam, with whom he has fallen in love.

The painfully humorous thing about the movie is that Greg knows Jack is one tough cookie who is scrutinizing his every move, just waiting for him to screw up. Of course, this pressure causes Greg to screw up even more. Mistakenly looking at an advertisement for breast pumps and then showing it to his potential father-in-law. Giving a fictional description during dinner conversation of how he milked a cat (complete with illustrative hand gestures). Destroying a cherished family urn with a champagne cork. Starting a fire in Jack's backyard the day before the wedding, after he had unknowingly flooded the yard with septic waste.

Jack was looking for Greg's mistakes, and that is exactly what he found.

Fishers of Great Things

This is how it often goes with parenting as well. With occasional exceptions, you usually find what you are looking for. I recently saw a news photo of a New Zealand fishing crew who pulled up a colossal squid—1,089 pounds and about the length of a school bus—from the Antarctic Ocean. Cool? Yes. A typical day in the life of your average sea bass fisherman? No. I imagine the average ratio of colossal squid to sea bass pulled up on those fishermen's nets is about 1:1,000,000,000,000,000. Why, you ask? Because they're not fishing for colossal squid. They're fishing for sea bass. While catching a colossal squid may break up the daily monotony for a while ("Look, he's eating the boat!"), sea bass is what pays the bills at the end of the week. And if you want to find sea bass, you have to know how to look for sea bass.

"What does all this have to do with me?" you might be asking right about now. "I'm not fishing for a colossal squid or for sea bass. In fact, I don't even live near a lake big enough to find either of them." Point well taken.* However, as dads, we are fishermen of a different sort. Jesus informed his disciples that they were to become "fishers of men" (Matt. 4:19). By this he meant that while they might continue to smell like raw fish, their lives would now be focused on declaring that God's kingdom had come and inviting others to share in this good news.

As dads, we are to become fishers of children. This does not mean you are to hang out around the local mall and grab other people's kids. So allow me to rephrase: you are

*I am indebted to my wife, who informed me that sea bass don't live in lakes.

to become a fisher of the great things in your children. This means you are to remember that your kids are God's workmanship, gold nuggets that he has created, and your job is to help them learn to shine.

Adjust Your Focus

If you are to become a fisher of the great things in your children, you have to be looking for the great things in your children. Here's a "Most Wanted" list of positive child traits and behaviors that hundreds of mothers and fathers have told me they are looking for:

- Doing what you ask them to do the first time
- Helping with a household task or chore in a friendly way (e.g., without complaining)
- Being "okay with it" if something doesn't go the way they want
- Telling the truth, even when it is hard to do
- Not giving up when something is hard
- Doing homework without making it a major ordeal
- Sharing something with a brother or sister

Most parents I know would actually pay money for their kids to do these things. In fact, they pay *me* to get their kids to do these things. The tragic secret: their kids are already doing many of them. At least sometimes. I guarantee it. But the parents have become so unconsciously focused on their children's negative behaviors that they honestly don't even remember the times when their children do something positive.

I've seen it happen before my very eyes. Connor was an eight-year-old, blond-haired young boy who was coming to see me because he didn't listen to his parents very often. To be more exact, he *never* listened to his parents. I had seen Connor a couple times already and had begun teaching him something I call "Fast Listening."[1] I had also talked with Mr. and Mrs. Johnson about the importance of watching for Connor's positive behaviors.

One afternoon, I walked out to the waiting room to retrieve Connor and his father. I opened up the waiting room door to see Connor and his father sitting there, playing checkers. Mr. Johnson saw me there and said, "Okay, let's clean up." Connor looked at me and smiled, and he immediately began dumping the checkers into their plastic container.

Great, I thought to myself. *He's already listening better.*

As we made our way to my office, I told Connor, "Nice job listening to your dad out there, pal," and gave him a little pat on the back. After we sat down, I asked Mr. Johnson how he had been doing with watching for Connor's positive behavior. "Well," he stated with a rather grim look on his face, "I'm looking, but he hasn't given me very much positive behavior to reward."

Do you see the problem? Connor had just listened *immediately* when his father asked him to put the checkers away. It was exactly the behavior the Johnsons wanted to see, and Connor had done it perfectly. Yet ninety seconds after it happened, Mr. Johnson had forgotten that it ever took place.

I see this problem all too often. Mr. Johnson had not yet adjusted his focus to zero in on Connor's positive behavior, and it was preventing him from having the kind of impact that a great dad can have. In other words, he wasn't being effective at fishing for the great things in his son. The good news is that over the next few weeks, Mr. and Mrs. Johnson both learned how to adjust their focus more effectively, and Connor's behavior improved dramatically.

If you want to adjust your focus, all you need to do is choose two or three positive behaviors or traits that you want to see more often. Sharing with a sibling. Working hard on homework. Washing and waxing your car. These are your sea bass. Now, when a sea bass fisherman sees a sea bass, he gets rather excited. So when you see these behaviors, let your kids know that you are excited about them. Then keep on looking for more, because as any good sea bass fisherman knows, where there is one sea bass, there are lots more just underneath the surface.

See Past the Mistakes

If we want to be great dads, not only do we need to adjust our focus to be on the lookout for our kids' positive attributes and behaviors, we also need to learn how to see past their mistakes. A mistake is an unintentional bad choice at best and a purposeful bad choice at worst. The truth is that your children, just like dear old dad, will make hundreds of mistakes. And that's just before breakfast. But our topic right now is not your children's mistakes but what you choose to *focus on* when they make those mistakes.

There's an old story about a boy who wanted to be the president of a bank. He walked up to the bank president and asked, "Sir, what do I need to do to become a bank president?" The bank president thought for a minute and then answered, "Two words: good choices." The boy asked, "How do I learn to make good choices?" The bank president responded, "One word: experience." The boy said, "Well, how do I get experience?" The bank president answered, "Two words: bad choices."

When your child argues about doing homework, acts like a poor sport when she loses a game of Monopoly, or lets the air out of the neighbor's tires in the middle of the night, what do you see? Do you see a kid who should have a permanent *L* taped to her forehead? Do you see someone whose future likely includes five to ten in San Quentin? Or are you able to see a great kid who made a bad choice?

A great dad will learn to look past the mistakes and see not only the great kid inside but also the potential for learning that each mistake holds. I want you to see your child's mistakes for what they really are: bad choices that can become rich learning experiences that will lay the foundation for good choices the next time around.

In my book *The Parent Survival Guide*, I tell the story of a boy I once knew, whom we'll call "sticky-fingers Louie."[2] Louie was a ten-year-old boy who had invited his friend Brian over to play with their trading cards. Brian had a "hard to get" card that Louie desperately wanted, and mysteriously that card went missing when he was at Louie's house (cue the music from *CSI*). Brian was sure that he had brought the card with him, but even with the help of Mrs. Olson, Louie's mom, they couldn't find it.

Well, a couple weeks later, Mrs. Olson was putting away the binder that Louie used for his cards when she saw a card sticking out of the inside pocket on the back cover. Upon closer examination, she realized that this was the card Brian had "lost." Busted. She waited until Mr. Olson got home, and they told Louie about their discovery that night.

Luckily for Louie, Mr. and Mrs. Olson did not have to resort to Jack Bauer–type interrogation tactics to get the truth out of him. He confessed right away that he had put the card in his binder when Brian stepped out to go to the bathroom. The Olsons realized that this was an opportunity to turn a big mistake into an even bigger learning experience for Louie.

Here's what they did. In addition to keeping Louie's own trading cards for a month, Mrs. Olson took Louie over to Brian's house the next day, where Louie gave Brian his card back, apologized, and told him that he hoped they could still be friends. He also handed Brian a brand-new pack of cards that he had bought with his own money. Later that week, Mr. Olson took some time with Louie to talk about the relationship consequences of stealing and why God warned us not to take things that aren't ours. By the way, to Louie's delight, Brian eventually called him and asked to play, and their friendship was restored.

Mr. and Mrs. Olson looked past Louie's mistake and saw a wonderful young boy who had made a poor, impulsive decision that they were able to translate into a wonderful life lesson. As a result of his parents' response to his mistake, Louie now had a new appreciation for the wisdom of the tenth commandment ("Thou shalt not covet thy neighbor's trading cards").

Try Bigger Glasses

Have you ever wondered how God looks at your children? What he thinks about them? Well, let's consider a couple basic facts. First, he made them, and that's rather important. Second, he has plans for them that include them being adopted into his family and spending a joyful eternity serving him.

That means that he made them to last. Forever. Now, nothing on this planet is made to last forever.* How long are things made to last down here? Until the day after the manufacturer's warranty expires. That's about it. Your kids were designed to spend *eternity* with God. That means they are made out of some seriously good material.

That's how God views your children: his personally designed little gold nuggets, made in his own image. Not chicken nuggets. Gold nuggets. Not perfect gold nuggets—far from it. Gold nuggets who, as part of a fallen creation, find it a lot easier to make a sinful choice than an obedient choice. Gold nuggets that need to surrender their lives to him. That have some dirt on them that needs brushing off. And God has given you the gold brush and said, "I'd like you to brush this nugget off. Bring out the pure gold that is inside." Johann Wolfgang von Goethe once wrote, "Treat people as if they were what they ought to be, and you help them to become what they are capable of being."[3] Let's tweak that quote a little to apply to us as fathers: "Look at your children the way that God looks at them, and you will help them become what God made them to be."

*With the exception of Styrofoam cups.

46

Gold nuggets.

Despite his mistakes, Greg Focker turned out to be a pretty good guy after all. In the same way, hidden beneath your child's mistakes is a gold nugget, handmade by God himself. And a great dad will learn to look for the gold. Even in the mistakes. Even on the bad days. It's always there. Sometimes it might be rather difficult to see, but it's never not there. Your kids need a dad who can see more in them than they see in themselves. How does he do this? By remembering something that is easy for them to forget: they are God's gold nuggets.

Key Points

1. You find what you are looking for.
2. God has called you to be a "fisher of great things" in your children.
3. It is important to adjust your focus so you can be immediately aware of your child's many positive traits and choices.
4. A great dad will look past his child's mistakes and turn them into great learning experiences.
5. Your children are God's handmade gold nuggets who still need a little (or a lot of) dusting off.

Getting to Work

1. Try this "fill in the blank" exercise:

Example	Lesson
1. Gaylord Focker	If you are looking for mistakes, then _____ are what you'll find.
2. Sea bass and colossal squid	If you want to find your child's positive behavior, then you have to _____ for your child's positive behavior.
3. Connor putting away his checkers	Your child displays more _____ behavior than you might think.

Example	Lesson
4. Louie stealing trading cards	Any mistake can be turned into a great _____.
5. Gold nuggets that need some brushing	When you look at your children the way that God does, you can help them become what _____ made them to be.

(**Answers:** 1. mistakes; 2. look; 3. positive; 4. lesson; 5. God)

2. Do you think you are more tuned in to your kids' negative behavior or their positive behavior? When you have been more tuned in to their negative behavior at times (and who hasn't?), what impact do you think that had on them? What impact will it have on them when you begin to look for the gold?

3. List three gold nugget behaviors you want to see your kids do more often. Determine to look for those behaviors like you were fishing for sea bass or mining for gold. What clues can you get from those two analogies (fishing and mining) that will help you find the great things in your kids?

4. Proverbs 10:11 tells us that "The mouth of the righteous is a fountain of life." Let's practice being a fountain of life when our child makes a mistake. Think of a specific mistake (e.g., bad choice) that your child has made in the past. Using that mistake as a practice example, think of how you could turn that bad choice into a good experience for your child that will lay the foundation for a better choice the next time around.

5. How will remembering that your kids are God's precious gold nuggets affect the way you respond to them when they make bad choices? When they make good choices?

Every Day Makes an Impact

One of our family's favorite things to do is to sit down in the family room and watch our DVR*-recorded episodes of the popular show *Whose Line Is It Anyway?* Hosted by comedian Drew Carey, this show features four talented improvisational comedians who perform hilarious games based on suggestions from the studio audience (occasionally requiring parental discretion). After each game, Carey pronounces a "winner" and awards the winner a random number of points, which really aren't used for anything.

Carey introduces the show by quipping, "This is the show where everything is made up and the points don't matter. That's right, the points are useless, just like . . . the talent portion of the Miss USA pageant" or "*TV Guide* on your wedding night."

*The best invention since toilet paper. Maybe better.

While the points don't matter on *Whose Line Is It Anyway?*, every moment you spend with your children does matter. Big time. In this chapter we'll focus not on how you think about your children but on how you think about the *time* you have with your children.

The Clock Is Running

This last weekend we attended the funeral for the father of one of Luke's basketball friends, Tony. Tony's father had succumbed to cancer. The church was packed with friends, loved ones, and children whom Jim had coached over the years, whose lives he had positively impacted. But the fact remains that fourteen-year-old Tony will spend the rest of his teenage years and all his adult life without a father to lean on or learn from.

Tony's story is not an isolated one. Sometimes the fathers leave the kids. Other times the kids leave the fathers. The longer you live, the more you are a witness to life's uncertainties.

Around three thousand years ago, King David was well aware of the shortness of life. In Psalm 103:15–16 he wrote, "As for man, his days are like grass, he flourishes like a flower of the field; the wind blows over it and it is gone, and its place remembers it no more."

As fathers, we don't have any guarantees about the number of days we will have with our children. However, we always have the guarantee of God's love and faithfulness, as David was quick to point out: "But from everlasting to everlasting the LORD's love is with those who fear him, and his righteousness with their children's children—with those who keep his covenant and remember to obey his precepts" (Ps. 103:17–18).

So when it is all said and done, what do we have that we can count on? We have God's love and faithfulness, and we have right now.

Make Every Day Count

Mark Twain captured the spirit of the everyday modern dad when he gave this immortal advice: "Never put off until tomorrow what you can do the day after tomorrow."[1] This maxim has been the guiding force behind the behavior of fathers for hundreds of years, and there is no doubt that Twain's wisdom holds true for virtually every situation a father encounters, except one—the impact they have on their kids. With that in mind, I would like to suggest that we break with tradition, fight our DNA, and adopt a new maxim: never put off until tomorrow the positive impact you can have on your kids today.

Here is a list of questions that every father should sequentially think through each morning before he gets out of bed. As soon as you have answered one question, you can move to the next, and so on:

1. "Whose house is this?"
2. "Where's my wallet?"
3. "Do I have any kids?"
4. "Do they know about me?"
5. "What kind of impact do I want to have on them today?"

Each day is an opportunity to shape your children's lives just a little bit more. Do you remember what we have talked about in the previous three chapters? Paying attention to the details of your kids' lives. Looking for the prizes God has hidden inside each of your children and finding ways to nurture those special traits. Seeing beyond your child's mistakes and capturing each one as a powerful learning opportunity. And finally, remembering that your kids are God's own handcrafted gold nuggets, made to live with him forever.

Every kid needs a dad who will make the most of these opportunities.

Not the day after tomorrow.
Today.

Seize the Times

In his book *Nurturing the Leader within Your Child*, Tim
Elmore gives some practical advice based on Deuteronomy
6:7.[2] Here's what this verse says:

> Impress [these commands] on your children. Talk about them
> when you sit at home and when you walk along the road,
> when you lie down and when you get up.

Elmore points out that this verse reminds us of four key
times we have every day for impacting our children: mealtimes, travel time, bedtime, and morning time. Let's take a
look at how a great dad can make the most impact in each one.
Mealtimes. In today's busy world, times when your family
is all together at once become increasingly scarce, especially
as your kids hit the teen years. This makes mealtimes all the
more special and important. While it is okay to watch TV
together during a meal now and then,* there are other ways
you can turn mealtimes into impact times.

For instance, you could spend your mealtimes brainstorm-
ing solutions to solve the Western hemisphere's slow decay of
Judeo-Christian ethics and subtle adoption of a postmodern
worldview within our educational and political systems.

Or you could just play the Question Game.

The Question Game starts with one person who gets to
ask any (appropriate) question they want, usually starting
with a rather simple question, such as, "What is your favorite
_____?" Starting with the person on the question-asker's
left and going around in a circle, each person gives a short
answer. Then the next person gets to ask a question, and so

*For instance, during football, basketball, baseball, hockey, lacrosse, golf,
tennis, ping pong, and motocross seasons.

on. The game moves rather quickly, which is part of what keeps it interesting and fun. Once you have done a couple rounds of lightweight questions, you can start to layer in more thought-provoking questions* such as, "What is something you are praying about?" "What is your favorite Bible verse?" or "What is one way you can make a difference at your work or school?" The game can end at any time or lead into a discussion that naturally stems from one of the questions.

The point is that mealtimes can be great impact times with your kids. Discussing a Scripture verse, having everyone give one highlight of their day, playing the Question Game, letting your kids hear you give your wife a compliment, asking about your kids' day or activities, helping clean up after dinner—all of these have as much impact potential as eating your veggies.

Travel times. Travel times are pretty much like mealtimes without the food—possibly better, because you have your kids in a space they can't escape without jumping through a car window. These are wonderful opportunities for making an impact in a fun way. Here are some of the travel time activities our family has enjoyed over the years:

- Reading jokes out of a joke book
- Playing travel games
- Listening to an audio book
- Discussing questions from *The Complete Book of Questions* by Gary Poole
- Talking about what's going on with your family, such as potential girlfriends, peer pressure, sharing their faith with friends, responding to negative peer behavior, allowances, and many other topics

I'll never forget the trip from California to Ohio that my dad and I took when Lora and I moved to the Midwest for

*If you have a juvenile delinquent, try this question: "If you were to hide drugs in the house, where would you hide them?"

my psychology internship in Dayton, Ohio. My dad and I took the twenty-four-foot U-Haul trailer, stuffed with every belonging we had and towing our Buick Skyhawk behind it. As we drove across the country in the dead heat of August, we reminisced about our family's experiences, and I learned many details about my dad's childhood in Canada. We talked about the beginning of my career as a psychologist and laughed together at funny trivia from *Uncle John's Bathroom Reader*.

Many years later, Dad told me that this trip was the most difficult thing he's ever gone through. Given my typical digestive reaction to Taco Bell drive-through food, this wasn't hard for me to imagine. But he was referring to driving his son 2,100 miles away and leaving him there. Being the father of two teenage boys, I now know what he meant, as envisioning that trip with my boys immediately fills my eyes with the same foreign, watery substance that I experience every year the Cowboys fail to make the playoffs. But neither Dad nor I would trade that trip for the world as it was a bonding time that each of us will remember forever.

Bedtimes. With our boys, bedtimes have been natural discussion opportunities. Whether it is the lack of distractions or the fact that they are starting to wind down, we have had some really great discussions spontaneously occur before our nightly prayers. A great dad is always watching for these moments and is willing to sacrifice whatever else he was going to do* when they pop up.

Bedtimes are also a great opportunity to pray with your kids. Sometimes, when my boys are in bed and I'm kneeling along the bedside, they pray out loud and I pray silently along with them. Other times, they will pray out loud, and then I'll follow by also praying out loud. Having done both, I think I like it best when we both pray out loud, for this not only gives me a chance to listen to and pray along with

---

*Such as reading up on how to build a *fast* Pinewood Derby car.

my boys but also gives them a chance to hear how their dad prays.

Morning times. Mornings are usually filled with the hustle and bustle of getting ready for school and work. Many dads I know are actually out of the house before their kids even wake up, while others are able to adjust their schedule so that they see their kids in the morning. I have done both. No matter what your morning situation is, there are a couple of ways you can turn the mornings into impact moments.

While dads are usually on the receiving end of Post-it notes, you can actually use these little "Honey-do list" vehicles for good by using them to let your kids know you haven't forgotten they exist. The Post-it notes that I leave for my kids usually have something to do with picking up the dog poop when they get home from school.* However, you can leave a Post-it note on the kitchen counter or on their bathroom mirror with a short, encouraging comment, such as:

- Love you. —Dad.
- Proud of you. —Dad.
- I'm praying for you today. —Dad.

The most important word in each note: Dad. That simple note that takes no more than ten seconds to write communicates that they are important enough to be on your mind. Mission accomplished.

Other morning ideas that make a big impact include praying together for the day to come, asking about what they have going on that day, and making physical contact with a hug or a squeeze on the hand, arm, or shoulder. Repeated every morning, these actions will fill your mornings with memories that your kids will end up telling your grandkids about.

*Typically complete with a beautifully hand-drawn illustration of you-know-what.

Count the Marbles

In *Nurturing the Leader within Your Child*, Tim Elmore tells the story of a man who did a little math. Based on a 75-year life expectancy, he figured that he had a total of 3,900 Saturdays, of which he had already lived 2,800. That left about 1,000 still to go. He bought 1,000 marbles and put them in a rather large container. Each Saturday, he removed one marble as a visual reminder to focus on the important things in life.[3]

This is a wonderful story and a great reminder about keeping our priorities in line. But there are two hidden lessons in this story. First, none of us are *guaranteed* 3,900 marbles. The truth is that some of us reading this book may have fewer marbles left in our jar than we think.

Second, we can make an impact on our kids *every* day, not just Saturdays. Over 75 years, that adds up to 27,375 marbles. That's a lot of marbles, and that's a lot of impact from a great dad. If you are in a position where you don't see your kids every day, due to work demands or divorce, then your job is to make the biggest impact you can on the days you have. Whether at mealtimes, travel times, morning times, bedtimes, or any other time, being fully aware that *every day* is a "marble" from God will help you make the life-giving impact on your children that only a great dad can make. And that's something that *will* matter for eternity.

Key Points

1. The clock is ticking on the time you have with your children.
2. Never put off until tomorrow the impact you can have on your kids today.
3. Mealtimes and travel times are great opportunities for both fun and meaningful discussions.

4. Bedtimes and morning times are great opportunities for praying together and staying connected through talking, notes, and physical touch.
5. God has given you a certain number of marbles, so make the best use you can of every single one.

Getting to Work

1. Do you know of a family where a father's time with his children was cut tragically short? If that father could talk to us now, what words of wisdom do you think he would offer?
2. Reflecting on all the chapters in section 1 (chapters 1–4), put into your own words the way God wants you to look at two things:
   a. your children
   b. the time you have with your children
3. List a few ways that you can start to include fun interactions and meaningful discussions in your mealtimes and travel times. What are some of the activities or discussion formats that have worked for you the best?
4. With your work and/or travel schedule, how can you make the best use of bedtimes and morning times with your children? How do you think regularly turning these daily times into impact moments will affect your children over the next five years?
5. Read Psalm 90:12; 103:14–18; and Ecclesiastes 7:2. The Bible reminds us that there is wisdom in being aware of our limited number of days. Keeping the jar of 1,000 marbles in mind, what lesser things are crowding in on your life and keeping you from making the impact God wants you to make on your children?

PART 2

Your Mouth

How You Talk to Your Children

When Dad Talks, Who Listens?

In the 1980s, the brokerage firm E. F. Hutton came out with several television commercials that pictured people walking and talking in everyday situations, such as walking through a park. The television lens then zeroed in on one particular conversation between two ordinary looking people. Suddenly, one of the men talking would say something like, "Well, my broker, E. F. Hutton, said . . ." At that point, all the people within earshot immediately stopped whatever it was they were doing or saying and craned their heads toward the man who had mentioned E. F. Hutton. When I saw these commercials, I liked to imagine planes freezing in midair and even little squirrels tilting their heads to hear if E. F. Hutton could give them any tips on walnut trading with China. The commercial's message was loud and clear: when E. F. Hutton talks, people (and small rodents) listen.

As dads who want to have a great impact on our children, we need to become great communicators. Let's think of communication as a friendly game of catch. The ball is the message that is being communicated. The goal of the communicator is to toss the ball (e.g., the message he wants to communicate) in a way that makes it easy for the other person to catch. In other words, he doesn't launch a 90 mph fastball at his listener. The goal of the listener is to focus on the ball (e.g., the message that is being communicated) so he can catch it.

In this chapter, we're going to focus on how you throw the ball to your kids. There are two main issues in great ball-throwing for dads. They are (1) what you talk about, and (2) how you talk about it.

What You Talk About

Little stuff. When I meet a new child I am going to work with, I always start our first interview with the same question. I ask them what they like to do for fun. They tell me they like to play outside with friends, play video games, and throw darts at the cat. I ask them about things they are good at, what they like about their family, and how often they actually hit the cat. It is only in the last quarter of our discussion that we start to talk about the main reason they have come to see me.

Now, I could start our discussion by asking why they argue with their parents, or about the divorce, or about any other big topic that I already know is the reason they are sitting in my office. But that would simply make them feel defensive and turn the volume on their headphones back up. In his book *Family First*, Phil McGraw found that of the seventeen thousand parents he surveyed, there was an inversely proportional relationship between the number of words spoken in the home and the amount of trouble the kids got into.[1] What does that mean in English? It simply means that the parents who spent more time talking with their kids had kids who got into trouble less. For you engineers, here's the algebraic breakdown: talking more with your kids = better relationship connection = kids getting in less trouble.*

And most of that talking is about little stuff.

Talking about the "little stuff" is important because it shows your kids that you really care about the details of their lives, which of course, is actually "big stuff" to them. So technically you could argue that there is no little stuff. Little stuff can include almost anything, such as current hobbies and interests, Fluffy the hamster's newest trick, or recent muggings at school. A dad who takes the time to show genuine interest in his kids' little stuff is laying the relational groundwork for talking about the big stuff, because his kids know that he really cares.

Big stuff. Sometimes kids bring up the big stuff. Often, they don't. That means it's up to you. In fact, your kids are secretly hoping that you will talk with them about the big issues. Despite what they may say, kids are well aware that they don't know it all, and they are trusting that you care enough to insert your guidance into their lives. Big stuff includes many topics that can be talked about regularly, such as friendships, dating, drugs, God, sex, and family relationship issues.

Let's flip it around for a second and think about the message you send to your kids if you *don't* talk with them about the big stuff. For instance, pretend that nine-year-old Renee comes home from school with a chain saw. She takes the chain saw up to her room and goes about her normal after-school business. Mom and dad both notice the chain saw, but neither of them mention it. What is Renee to think? She knows that bringing a chain saw into the house is a big deal. She knows that any parent with even a gerbil-sized brain should question her about the chain saw. Yet her parents don't say a word. The message is unmistakable: either her parents don't care, or they have no idea what a chain saw is.

---

* = less chance of winding up on *The Jerry Springer Show.*

I remember in sixth grade when my dad drove me to the local A&W drive-in and ordered us both a root beer. My Canadian instincts told me that something was coming, and I was right. The birds and the bees talk. Big stuff. I don't exactly remember much of what my dad told me, which is probably why it took Lora and me so long to get pregnant the first time. I do remember that I was rather grossed out. But it didn't really matter. My dad had taken the time to talk with me about something big, and I appreciated it.

Then I threw up.

How You Talk about It

Solomon tells us, "The mouth of the righteous is a fountain of life" (Prov. 10:11). Here are a few communication tips for *how* to talk about both the little and big things with your kids in a way that will be a fountain of life for your family:

1. *Choose the right time and setting.* The Bible reminds us that there is "a time to be silent and a time to speak" (Eccles. 3:7). This is a good verse to keep in mind when there is a difficult subject to talk about or when your wife is asking if it was you or the dog who put the red football jersey in the wash with her new white blouse.*

With your kids, a good topic brought up at the wrong time is about as welcome as a Hawaiian pig roast at a bar mitzvah. If you have a specific topic you need to discuss, tell your child *in advance* that you both need to sit down and discuss it. "Buddy, we need to sit down together and talk about music and how to make the right choices about what to listen to, okay? How about if we do it tomorrow, after dinner? That will give both of us time to get our ideas together so our discussion can be a good one." This advance notice gives your child time to think about what he wants to say, treats

---

*Correct answer: it was the dog.

him respectfully by giving him time to think about it, and gives you a chance to thoughtfully and intelligently prepare your end of the conversation.

The setting of the conversation is equally important, especially with kids who put up an invisible force field whenever you start to talk to them. Whenever I have a child in my office who has made it abundantly clear that he would rather be scraping barnacles off the bottom of a boat with his tongue than sitting in my office, I quickly shift gears and have us play a game to reduce the awkward pressure to talk. Engaging in a fun activity creates a relaxed backdrop where a casually paced conversation can naturally develop. In our family, I have found that activities such as playing a video game, shooting baskets, playing a game such as Battleship or chess, or even cleaning up the basement* have created a "relaxed conversation environment" that made it easy for us to casually talk about school, friends, God, or a home situation in an enjoyable and productive way.

2. *Use "I-statements."* I have found that the way a dad phrases his thoughts is every bit as important as the thoughts themselves. At the risk of making you sound like Sigmund Freud Jr., one effective way to express your thoughts and ideas is to use "I-statements." They work much better than their evil counterparts: "You-statements." Take a look at these examples:

You-statement	I-statement
"Your room looks like a pig sty."	"Jason, I would really appreciate it if you would clean up your room when I ask you to."
"You need to drop that tone."	"Gina, I really don't like it when you talk with that kind of a tone. It makes it difficult for us to have a good conversation."

---

*All of these activities are almost always more effective when done *with* your kids.

You-statement	I-statement
"You're late again!"	"Adam, I've noticed that the last several times you've come home, it's been about fifteen minutes after the time we agreed upon. We need to find a way to fix that."

Notice that the I-statements use your child's first name, which helps to reinforce the idea that you actually *know* your child's first name. They also calmly state the facts (or your feelings) and move the discussion in a solution-focused direction, rather than using critical accusations that put your child on the defensive. Finally, if you do a little arithmetic, you will see that each I-statement contains more words than its You-statement counterpart, which communicates three important things: (1) you still remember how to do arithmetic, (2) a certain amount of actual thought was put into your sentence, and (3) you want to *talk* about the topic together, rather than *yell* about it together.

3. *Develop a warm communication style.* For some of you, a warm communication style just comes naturally; for others of you it doesn't. No problem. Just start where you are and begin to develop it. A warm communication style will make you an "easy to listen to" kind of dad, which is much better than being a "hard to listen to" kind of dad, just in case you were wondering.

I remember talking recently with Luke about a girl he likes and was interested in "going out with." However, due to the fact that he was not yet past the ripe old age of fourteen, Luke did not exactly get the answer he was hoping for from me. As we sat on his bed and talked about it, Luke asked some very good questions about why Lora and I didn't want him to date yet, and I did my best to answer them as honestly and thoroughly as I could.* However, the main thing that sticks in my memory about that discussion was that Luke and I were able to talk through it in a warm and positive way.

*I told him all girls are secretly vampires.

One of the reasons that Luke and I were able to have a positive discussion that night was because I kept a warm communication style throughout our discussion. A warm communication style sends the great dad message: *I know this topic is important to you and I want to make sure we talk about it together the right way.* Funny thing is that when *you* keep a warm communication style, it often helps your kids do the same.

One thing that helps me maintain a warm communication style with both of my boys is to keep in mind how valuable they are to me, which prompts me to make sure I do everything I can to keep a warm relationship connection—no matter what we are talking about. While this can be a tall order sometimes, it is usually not too hard to do. All you have to do is use the following guide to see how you can turn a "hard to listen to" communication style into an "easy to listen to" style that will keep your kids coming back for more:

Hard to listen to	Easy to listen to
Yells	Warm tone of voice
Put-downs	Encouraging
Interrupts	Listens to child's feelings
Focuses on the negative	Focuses on positive ideas or solutions
Reactive	Firm but self-controlled
Longwinded	Short, engaging comments
Irritated tone and angry look	Positive physical touch and warm smile
Randomly talks about power tools	No mention of power tools

Using this guide, take a minute to do a personal inventory on your communication style. While all of us will make communication mistakes from time to time, does your typical communication style have more in common with the "hard to listen to" or "easy to listen to" list?

Keeping a warm communication style as Luke and I talked about his dating future helped keep our conversation encouraging and productive. Of course, all of the "easy to listen to" tips above can be inserted into *any* conversation you have with your kids (even the hard ones) and will help your communication to stay positive and supportive.

Whether talking about the little stuff or the big stuff, a great dad will learn how to communicate positively and effectively with his kids. Choosing the right time and setting, using I-statements, and developing a warm communication style will turn you into a dad that your kids will *want* to talk to. And want to listen to. Even more than E. F. Hutton.

Key Points

1. Talking about the "little stuff" communicates that you care about the details of your child's life and opens the door for talking about bigger issues.
2. Your kids are counting on you to talk to them about the "big stuff" on a regular basis.
3. The right time and a relaxed setting can help your conversation feel more natural and be more productive.
4. Using I-statements communicates that you want to talk together about an issue in a thoughtful and respectful way.
5. A great dad will develop a warm communication style that makes him an "easy to listen to" kind of dad.

Getting to Work

1. How would you describe the strengths and weaknesses of your communication style in talking with your kids?
2. Read Philippians 2:3–4. As dads, it is so easy to get caught up with the nonstop demands of work and family activities that we forget about the little and big things happening in our kids' lives. Remembering Paul's

admonition to be thoughtful of "the interests of others" (v. 4), how can you show your kids that you are interested in the little and big things going on in their lives right now?

3. What settings have helped you to have positive conversations with your kids? What was it about those settings that made them helpful?

4. To many of us, I-statements don't feel natural, but then again, neither does folding laundry. So if you can learn to fold laundry, you can learn to make I-statements.* Taking the three examples given on pages 65–66 (messy room, negative tone, coming in late), what I-statement responses would you come up with? How do I-statements make it easier for your kids to listen to you?

5. Read Proverbs 12:18. Now read the list of "hard to listen to" and "easy to listen to" communication characteristics on page 67. Which of these lists best describes your daily communication with your kids? Take a pencil or highlighter and mark two or three characteristics from the "easy to listen to" list that you want to make a regular part of your communication style with your kids. What difference will it make if you do?

---

*By the way, you can learn to make I-statements even if you can't fold laundry.

Send a Message

I like to read. Usually my books of choice are either Christian apologetics (e.g., C. S. Lewis) or related to my work as a child psychologist (e.g., *Prenatal Toilet Training*). However, there is one book series that has become my favorite. It is filled with mystery, intrigue, betrayal, adventure, breathtaking battles, villains, superheroes, and time travel—all the ingredients that every boy longs for.

Captain Underpants.

One of the features I enjoy (and there are many in the Captain Underpants series[1]) is when the main characters, two likable but mischievous young boys named George and Harold, happen to come across any school bulletin board that has movable letters. The boys just can't restrain themselves from moving the letters around to create a new message. Here are a few of my favorites:

Old Message	New Message
DON'T UNDERESTIMATE OUR GOOD TEACHERS	OUR TEACHERS DON'T USE DEODORANT
HAVE A BLISSFULLY GRAND RETIREMENT, MS. RIBBLE	MS. RIBBLE REALLY NEEDS A BREATH MINT
SEE OUR BIG FOOTBALL GAME	BOY OUR FEET SMELL BAD
PLEASE WASH YOUR HANDS AFTER USING THE TOILET	PLEASE WASH YOUR HANDS IN THE TOILET

Even as a grown adult (and I use this term loosely), I am unable to avoid the involuntary snicker this type of preadolescent humor brings to my face. George and Harold remind me of my own Canadian elementary school prankster days. For instance, I remember bringing a fake mouse to school in fourth grade to scare my innocent, young, female teacher, Mrs. Stewart. I walked up to her desk with the mouse that I "caught" and accidentally dropped it on her. Funny. Until report card day.

Ah, the good old days. Well, just as George and Harold were masters at making changes in letters and words to create entirely new messages for the student body, a great dad knows how to use his words to send the right messages to his children. Messages far more important than Ms. Ribble's need for a breath mint. Messages that will resonate in their hearts and minds forever.

From Your Mouth to Your Child's Brain

How exactly do your words make their impact on your child's gray matter? If you were to ask your wife, here is the way she would diagram it:

1. Father has an original thought.
2. Father forgets thought.
3. Thought randomly reappears three weeks later.
4. Father quickly speaks thought (before he loses it again).

5. Mother hears father's thought.
6. Mother corrects father's thought.
7. Father restates mother's corrected version of his original thought.
8. Child hears mother's corrected version of father's original thought.
9. Child is convinced that father is all-knowing and wise.
10. Mother allows this delusion to continue as long as father continues to mow the lawn and take out the trash.

This, however, is incorrect. This diagram assumes that the father actually had an original thought, which research has proven to be untrue. Everything a father thinks comes from something he has either seen on television or read in *Sports Illustrated*. All joking aside, here is the actual diagram of how a father's words impact his child*:

1. Father has a thought.
2. Father speaks his thought, thus turning his thought into words.
3. Father's words enter child's ears.
4. Father's words make their way to child's brain.
5. Father's words are given high value as being true and mingle with child's own thoughts.
6. Father's words shape child's beliefs about himself or herself.
7. Child's beliefs about himself or herself shapes future choices and actions.
8. Father's words shape child's future.

It doesn't get any bigger than this. Because you're a father, your words have the power of dynamite. From the day your children are born, they instinctively trust your love and rely on your wisdom. After all, you're their dad, the alpha male

*Never, I repeat, never show this to your wife.

72

in their life. In their minds, what you say *must* be true simply because it comes from you. Especially when it is about them.

The way your children think about themselves will open or close worlds of opportunity, because their inner thoughts will drive their outer actions. A great dad will remind his children of the greatness that God has placed inside of them and will profoundly impact their tomorrows through the power of his words today.

Unleash Your Power

In the Captain Underpants books, all the students in George and Harold's school would pass by the bulletin board every day, reading the humorous messages that the boys had left for them to see. In the same way, you are a living bulletin board that your children read every day. With that in mind, here are three ways you can send messages straight from your heart to shape the way your children think about themselves from the inside out:

1. *Point out positive choices.* Your children make many positive choices each day. On some days, you might need the Hubble Space Telescope to find them, but they're there. Pointing them out sounds like a simple idea, but it makes a huge impact because it reminds your kids of who *you* think they are: God's gold nuggets. As Mother Teresa put it, "Kind words can be short and easy to speak, but their echoes are truly endless."[2] Here are a few examples of how you can encourage your kids when they make a positive choice:

- "Hey, Holly, great job on that research paper. You're turning into an awesome student!"
- "Alex, thanks for taking the dog out. That really shows me you're trying to help out."
- "David, your tuba playing is really coming along!"*

* You get extra "Great Dad" points for this one.

73

Positive, encouraging words are the bread and butter of a close father-child relationship, not the occasional steak sandwich. I suspect that most dads think they are fairly encouraging to their kids already. Of course, in their own minds, most dads also think they could double as a real-life James Bond, if given the chance. So, the issue isn't so much whether *you* think you are encouraging to your kids; it is whether your *kids* think you are encouraging to your kids.

How can you make sure that your kids will think they have the most encouraging dad on this side of the galaxy? Just ask them to tell you a few things that they are working on right now (such as an upcoming test, a music recital, writing your signature on school notes), or find out if there are any challenges they are facing so that you can be praying for them and encouraging them as they make positive choices in these areas. (Bedtimes are great for this.) When you point out the positive choices your kids make *every day*, even the little ones, they will feel noticed and appreciated and will give you even more positive choices to find.

2. *Point out positive attributes.* I once heard the story of a young couple, Stan and Connie, who were taking a walk one sunny afternoon. As they were walking, Connie asked Stan, "Do you think my eyes are beautiful?"

Stan answered, "Yes, I do."

A couple minutes later, Connie asked, "Do you think my hair is attractive?"

Stan responded, "Yes, I do."

"Do you think I have a gorgeous figure?"

"Yes, I do."

"Oh Stan," Connie beamed, "you say the nicest things."[3]

Lucky for us guys, encouraging words don't have to be long and fancy in order to make a big impact. I recently noticed that Luke had been making a lot of effort to be a good influence with his friends, both through his behavior and by inviting them to youth group activities. So as we were heading out to throw a football one afternoon, I took the opportunity to tell him how proud I was of his desire to positively impact his friends.

"Hey pal," I said, "I've noticed that you've been inviting kids to youth group and have been really trying to be a good friend and example to them. That shows me that you're really trying to be the kind of friend that God wants you to be. I'm really proud of you for that—you're doing a great job." It didn't take long to say, but the look on his face told me that it had registered. Just like watering a young plant, pouring out those five seconds of positive encouragement reminded Luke of two important things: (1) he was choosing to obey God by being a good friend, and (2) his dad noticed.

In her book *Strong Fathers, Strong Daughters*, Meg Meeker emphasizes the special importance a father's positive words have in the life and development of his daughter. Meeker encourages dads to make a special effort to focus their words on their daughter's *inner* qualities and positive attributes. Girls will treasure every positive communication they receive from their dads in the form of positive comments and even little love notes.* She writes, "Reflect on your daughter's character, praise her best attributes, talk about her sensitivity, compassion, or courage. Your daughter will draw a picture in her mind of how *you* see her, and that's the person she'll want to be."[4]

3. *Point out positive results.* Robert Sinclair wrote, "We don't really learn anything from our experience. We only learn from reflecting on our experience."[5] While our children make many positive choices each day, most kids I know don't often stop to *reflect* on the positive results of these choices, and as a result, they miss the lesson of how their positive choices have paid off.

For instance, my sixteen-year-old son, Jake, has taken a very slow and thoughtful approach to the area of girls and

*Yes, great dads write love notes.

girlfriends.* We have talked at length about the pros and cons of having a girlfriend, what dating even means, and what type of girl *friend* he should even consider dating. We've talked about the critical importance of seeking God's guidance regarding girls and dating, as Proverbs 3:5–6 tells us to "Trust in the LORD with all your heart and lean not on your own understanding; in all your ways acknowledge him, and he will make your paths straight." To keep a long story short, Jake has made some very good decisions in this area and has thus far had dating relationships with two lovely Christian girls (both of whom had clean FBI background checks). I have clearly seen Jake's desire to handle all aspects of dating in a way that keeps him solidly on God's path.

Not too long ago, we were sitting on his bed before saying our nightly prayers, and I had a chance to tell him how proud I was of how he was handling this challenging area of teenage life. We reflected together on the benefits Jake has experienced (the good results that have happened to him and the bad results he has avoided) as the result of staying on God's path, and there were many. It wasn't difficult to think of examples of other teens Jake knew who had made poor decisions regarding the opposite sex and the variety of negative outcomes that had entered their lives as a result. In our prayers that night, we thanked God together for the blessings he gives to those who stay on his path.

In the same way, you can take the time to point out to your children the positive results of staying on God's path, even when other kids don't. This includes the benefits of being:

- a good friend
- honest
- respectful
- consistent in prayer and Bible reading
- hard working

*Behavior shock therapy was quite helpful as well.

The list could go on. When you help your children reflect on their choices to obey God and the many benefits they bring, both to themselves and others, it helps them realize that God's path is truly the best path, and they will be even more encouraged to be faithful in making positive, God-honoring choices in the future.

Dads, we have to remember that our words are even more powerful than a cafeteria bulletin board with George and Harold's rearranged letters. As a great dad in the making, use your words to send powerful messages that will echo in your kids' minds and hearts as you remind them of the positive choices they make, the positive attributes they are developing, and the positive results that God has promised to those who stay on his path. That message is a lot better than CABBAGE AND TURNIPS ON FRIDAY (Translation: BARF AND BUNS TODAY).

Key Points

1. A father's words send messages to his children every day.
2. Your words shape your children's beliefs about themselves and as a result, shape their lives.
3. Pointing out your children's positive choices encourages them to make even more.
4. Pointing out your children's positive attributes reminds them of the special gifts and qualities that God is developing in them.
5. Pointing out the positive results of staying on God's path will help your children appreciate the blessings and safeguards that God so faithfully promises to those who obey him.

Getting to Work

1. On a scale of 1 to 10, how encouraging do you think you are to your kids? What number would you like to be, and what do you need to do differently to get there?

2. Most parents I meet notice the big things their kids do right (i.e., saving the human race from nuclear annihilation within twenty-four hours), but they take for granted the little things (i.e., saving Nebraska). What would happen if you started giving your children daily encouragement for the "little" positive choices they make every day? How would that encouragement impact your family?

3. List one positive attribute for each of your children (see page 37 for ideas) and plan a time when you will positively encourage them about that attribute.

4. Read Proverbs 4:11 and 22:5. With these two Scripture verses in mind, identify what the benefits of staying on God's path have been for your own life. What blessings have you experienced as a result of staying on God's path? What snares and thorns has God kept you safe from? What has happened to you when you have strayed off of God's path? After considering these questions for yourself, find a time when you can discuss these three questions with each of your children (or together as a family) to help them reflect on the blessings they have experienced as a result of staying on God's path.

5. When you regularly point out your kids' positive choices, attributes, and results, what messages are you sending them?

Watch Out for Hazards

Last year I read an ABC News report that proclaimed that potholes cost United States drivers millions of dollars in car repairs. I have no problem believing that after I had my own unpleasant encounter with a Chicago-style pothole last winter. The front half of my car actually disappeared from sight for a second as my car lunged into and out of this monstrous gap in the road on my way to work one freezing Chicago morning. Amazingly, my right front tire (which took the brunt of the hit) was actually okay, but from that second on, the front part of my car made a strange groaning noise whenever I turned the steering wheel.

My solution, of course, was to simply stop making turns for as long as I could, which worked for a while.* When I finally did take my car in to the shop, my mechanic friend, Kevin, told me that some type of bar had actually snapped.

*Except it made my commute three hours longer.

I figured that was bad. Then I paid him a lot of money to fix that bar. That was worse.

Communication Hazards

In this chapter, we're going to talk about the potholes of father-child communication. Let's call them communication hazards for short. The definition of a hazard is something that causes unavoidable danger or risk, which is exactly why I stay as far away as possible from the laundry. Communication hazards are like potholes in three ways:

1. Even great dads stumble into them.
2. They can cause significant and costly damage.
3. If you learn how to watch for them, they can be avoided.

To soften the blow to our already fragile male egos, I have chosen to focus on only the three communication hazards that I witness most often. This may be a tough chapter to read because no one likes to look at their own bad habits. But in his take-no-prisoners style, Jesus told us to take the plank out of our eye before we try to remove a speck from our brother's eye (see Matt. 7:3–5). So, in the spirit of a football player studying his game tapes, looking for things to improve because he wants to be the best, I encourage you to take an honest look at your communication style and see if any of these hazards are slowing you down.

Hazard #1: Yelling

Now, I get being mad. It's a built-in part of being a parent. The question is: How are you going to handle the words that come out of your mouth when you're mad? When I talk with parents, I sometimes get the idea that they think they get a pass on yelling. Survey says . . . not a chance. I don't have to go farther than the Golden Rule—"Do unto others the way you would have them do unto you," or should I say, "*Talk* to others the way you would have them talk to you" (Luke 6:31, my paraphrase)—to remind myself that yelling is not the way God wants me to communicate with my kids.

Yelling is simply taking some words or ideas that may (or may not) actually be useful and communicating them in a way that makes them hard to listen to. It's like shaking hands with someone who has a shock buzzer concealed in his palm. You don't want to keep your hand connected very long because it's just plain unpleasant. I cannot think of a time when I've seen a parent yell at their child in my office and I thought, *Good for them. It's about time they started yelling.*

In fact, I met a nine-year-old girl recently in my office. As our initial interview unfolded, I eventually asked her about her family. Here's what she had to say:

Me: Okay, Leah, let's talk about your family. How do you and Mom get along?

Leah: Fine.

Me: So, you guys are pretty close?

Leah: Yeah.

Me: Well, what about you and Dad?

Leah: Not as close.

Me: Why is that?

Leah: He yells a lot.

Me: What does he yell about?

Leah: Homework. [Pause] Or if he's had a bad day.

That's Leah's perception of her dad. I had met Leah's dad one time previously and he seemed like a nice guy.* But his daughter, who knows him far better than I, described a damaged relationship with her dad, and the main reason in her mind was crystal clear: Dad yells. A lot.

*He didn't yell at me.

81

I can hear what you're thinking right now. *You mean I can't even raise my voice at my kids? You're taking all the fun out of being a dad!* Correction: I didn't say you can't raise your voice. In fact, there is a helpful distinction between yelling and raising your voice. Here's your comparison shopping guide:

Yelling	Raising Your Voice
Shows poor anger control	Shows self-control
Several levels louder than normal voice	Only "a notch" louder than normal voice
Face turns red	Normal face color
Veins pop out of neck	No veins
Often accompanied by evil look	Look no worse than if mildly constipated

If your normal voice level is a 4 on a scale of 1 to 10, with 1 as a whisper and 10 the type of screaming you would do at the March Madness Finals, then raising your voice would be around a 5 or 6 volume level. It's strong enough to communicate that you mean business but moderate enough to communicate a sense of self-control and thoughtful intention in your words. Yelling is a 7 or higher. To help you get the feel for respectfully raising your voice, read the following sentence to yourself:

If you say that one more time, I'm going to wet my pants.

First I want you to say this sentence at a normal "4" voice level. (Come on, really say it.) Listen carefully to how you sound. Then say the sentence again, staying at a 4 volume level but making your tone sound much more serious, like you *really* mean it. It's amazing the amount of seriousness your tone can add without even increasing the volume. Now say the sentence one more time, this time with a serious (but controlled) tone and the volume level at a 5. Can you hear the difference between a calm 4 and a serious 5? Now try a 9. Do you see how yelling actually *reduces* the quality of your communication? Kids understand their dad occasionally raising his voice; it's the yelling that shuts down the communication freeway.

Hazard #2: Put-Downs

Our family has enjoyed traveling to attend Luke's basketball games for the past several years. Basketball has given us the chance to discuss many important things, such as hard work, good sportsmanship, and how to make "yo momma" jokes when the referee is out of earshot.

Because I am a strong believer in practicing hard to reach your goals and want Luke to make the most out of every game (win or lose), he and I usually talk about his games afterward, identifying where he played well and any areas he could still improve on. During one such discussion, I had given Luke the feedback that he had not "driven the lane"* on several opportunities when I clearly thought he should have. Having talked with Luke about this many times before, I suspect my frustration was apparent, because I really did want him to improve his basketball skills.

As I gave him my best ESPN analysis, I could see Luke's face cloud over and his interest in my opinion come to a grinding halt. Something inside me told me I had blown it. A few hours later that same day, I asked Luke if he thought I had come on too strong or been too negative with my feedback. I inwardly winced as I anticipated his answer. "Yeah," Luke replied. "You didn't say anything positive. All you pointed out is what I did wrong."

Unfortunately, he was right. Without intending to, I had put my wonderful son down, and I had hurt our relationship. I squeezed Luke on the shoulder and told him that I was very sorry and hadn't meant to come across in such a negative

---

*Basketball lingo that I picked up from TV. I have no idea what it means.

way. His face immediately unclouded, and the lines of communication were reopened again between us.

The same type of "put-down effect" can happen with careless words. I have heard parents use words like *stupid*, *lazy*, *slob*, and *jerk* to describe their kids or their kids' behavior. The problem was that their kids were right there with us in my office when the parents used those words. Even worse is that 90 percent of the times I've heard parents use those name-calling words, they did not apologize, even when their child was clearly offended or hurt. Instead, they backpedaled (e.g., "You know I didn't mean that—what, are you stupid?") or tried to justify their comment by pointing to all the evidence that their child was a slob or really did act like a jerk.

The Bible tells us, "Do not let any unwholesome talk come out of your mouths, but only what is helpful for building others up according to their needs" (Eph. 4:29). Put-downs and name-calling are hazards of the first degree and, if repeated often, will have damaging effects on your child's self-esteem and your relationship connection. To help you avoid these hazards in the future, here are a couple nifty ideas:

1. *Use the Oreo method.* When giving constructive feedback, think of an Oreo cookie. Say one positive thing, then point out one area for improvement, and finish up by mentioning another positive thing. Remember to point out the area for improvement the way you'd like someone to do it for you. Positive, constructive, positive. All you need is milk.

2. *Describe the behavior.* If you don't want your discussion to take on the flavor of an ice hockey brawl, try simply *describing* the problem behavior to your child ("Pal, there are over twenty clothing items on the floor of your room, and I think I just saw one of them move") rather than throwing around emotionally loaded words (e.g., slob, stupid) that come across as insults. Remember,

84

your child isn't a slob; he's a gold nugget who needs to learn to pick up his clothes.

Hazard #3: Teasing

Words can be confusing. For instance, comedian Steven Wright tells a joke about naming his dog Stay. He says, "It's fun to call him. 'Come here, Stay! Come here, Stay!' He went insane. Now he just ignores me."[1]

Michelle was a fourteen-year-old girl I saw several years ago. One of the topics we discussed was her anger toward her father. Now, her father was a nice guy who loved his daughter. However, he repeatedly called her the little "baby name" that he had given her when she was a toddler. Now that she was fourteen years old, this name had lost its cute appeal for Michelle, who felt extremely embarrassed when he called her this name around her friends. Michelle had asked her dad to stop many times, but he didn't take the hint. Michelle knew that her dad loved her, but she was hurt and confused by his decision to continue teasing her in this way.

Proverbs 12:18 reminds us that "Reckless words pierce like a sword." Teasing comments or behaviors are communication hazards because they are hurtful. They damage your parent-child relationship and send a negative message to the core of your child's self-view. The question your child is left holding is: *Why would someone who loves me tease me like that?*

The solution to this hazard is to ask yourself two questions:

1. *How would I like it if . . . ?* Then fill in the blank with the behavior you are wondering about. For example, "How would I like it if someone kept teasing me in a certain way after I asked them not to?" or "How would I like it if my dad called me 'Big Boy' (and I was a little overweight) or made jokes at my expense?" The answer is obvious.

2. *Did my joke or comment have the intended positive effect?* If your good-intentioned joke or comment was received as being funny and supportive, then you'll see a smile or other positive signals that your child took your comments in a humorous and relationship-building way. If you're not sure, it's always a good idea to check. However, if your comment was not positively received by your child, it will be quickly followed by body language that will reveal hurt instead of humor. A lack of response, a sad or hurt expression, a direct comment (e.g., "Dad, that's not funny."), slumped shoulders, walking away— these all indicate that your joke missed its mark.

Bottom line, there is no discipline issue, basketball pointer, or joke that is more important to me than my relationship with Jake or Luke. I suspect that you feel the same way about your kids. If you find that the way you address negative behavior, give feedback, or joke around hurts your relationship with your kids, then you have stepped into a communication pothole. The way out is to immediately and genuinely apologize to your child and find another way to address negative behavior, give feedback, or joke around. In Chicago, most potholes can be avoided if you get in the habit of watching for them. In the same way, you can learn to spot and stay away from these three communication hazards and save your family a costly repair bill.

Key Points

1. Communication hazards are like potholes: anyone can hit them, they do costly damage, and they can be avoided.
2. Yelling shuts down productive communication just like a shock buzzer makes a handshake unpleasant.
3. Raising your voice to a 5 or 6 in a controlled way communicates seriousness along with a sense of respect and self-control.

4. You can avoid accidental put-downs by (a) using the Oreo method and (b) describing your child's negative *behavior* instead of using name-calling words.
5. Using the *"How would I like it if . . . ?"* question and paying attention to your child's reaction to jokes and funny comments will help your humor be a relationship-builder instead of a relationship-breaker.

Getting to Work

1. Which of these three communication hazards (if any) did your dad commit with you on a regular basis when you were a kid? How have these hazards (or the fact that your dad avoided them) impacted you both as a boy and now as a dad?
2. All of us have yelled at times, but some yell more than others. How would you rate yourself on a 1 to 10 yelling scale? What impact does your yelling (or lack of yelling) have on the relationship between you and your kids?
3. Think of a time when you put down your child, either intentionally or unintentionally. Replay that situation in your mind, imagining yourself either using the Oreo method or describing the behavior. What would the impact be on your child when you avoid the hazard?
4. Have you ever met anyone whose jokes and "teasing" go over the line? Is this a hazard you fall into? Which of the two questions listed in the teasing section will you use to avoid this hazard?
5. Read Ephesians 4:1–3, 29–32. What do these passages tell us about communication hazards? When you do fall into a communication hazard, how do you think God wants you to address it with your child?

Your Secret Weapon

Williham Wallace. Every time I say that name, I grow another chest hair. Just the mention of his name should create a stir of emotion in any man's heart. Or should I say his bowels. Either way, he was the Scottish keeper of the Man Cards. And he knew a thing or two about surprise battlefield tactics as well.

One of my favorite scenes from the movie *Braveheart*, which tells the Hollywood version of Scotland's fight for freedom from English rule in the late thirteenth century, took place on a large field on a cloudy day just outside of Sterling, Scotland. The English army had been dispatched by Edward Longshanks to quell the rebellion of a ragtag group of Scots led by Wallace. The problem for Wallace and his men was that they were heavily outnumbered, and as if that wasn't bad enough, the English had three hundred heavy horses* that would be used to mow down the Scots like grass.

---

*Complete with riders and long, nasty spears.

88

But Wallace had a secret weapon. A creative military genius, he had envisioned using spears "twice as long as a man" in a situation such as this. Wallace and his men had brought dozens of these spears to the front lines at Sterling and concealed them in the grass, out of sight of the English. Wanting to end the battle as quickly as possible, the English commanders sent in their horses to steamroll Wallace and his men. As far as the English were concerned, they would be able to easily finish this battle by lunch and be home in time to watch the Redskins play the Cowboys.

Picture yourself standing on a football field with three hundred "Refrigerator Perrys"* running toward you at full speed. This was the position Wallace and his men were in as the English horses reached full gallop and thundered toward them, bringing certain bone-crunching death. Wallace had his men hold their stance as long as possible, until it would be too late for the horsemen to slow down or change direction. At the last possible second, he gave the signal and the front line of Scots dropped to their knees and grabbed their long and powerful spears, creating a deadly destination for the English riders and their horses. Against all odds, Wallace and his men defeated the English army that day, and his secret weapon made it all possible.

The Power of Your Attention

Wallace's military accomplishments against armies with superior training and weaponry were remarkable, but what he wouldn't have given for a B-2 stealth bomber. Well, you have no such problem, as you have a secret weapon you didn't even know about. It's your attention. And your words are the delivery system. In chapter 6 I showed you how to use your words to shape your children's inner view of themselves.

---

*A 350+ pound defensive lineman from the 1985 Super Bowl champion Chicago Bears.

In this chapter I want to show you how to use your words to package your attention in a way that will influence their outer behavior. That's right: a great dad influences his kids from the inside out and the outside in.

Your attention is powerful because it sends many important messages to your children:

- I am important.
- I am loved.
- My dad notices me.
- If dad notices me, then I must be valuable to him.

These messages are affirming and highly reinforcing. In other words, everyone likes to feel noticed, valued, and important. Now, we want your kids to *always* know how important they are to you. But you will find that little "extra doses" of this type of attention have a powerful impact on your children's behavior. The beauty of it all is that you have an unlimited supply of this type of ammo, and I'm going to show you how to use it to help your kids learn that making good choices is a lot more fun than making bad ones.

The Pour It On Technique

I want to introduce you to something I call "The Pour It On Technique." A mom I just taught this to calls it "The Lay It On Thick Technique." I think I'll stick with the original title. When used properly, this laser-beam focused technique can have an amazingly positive impact on your children's behavior. I've seen it happen hundreds of times, even with very difficult children. Let me show you how it works.

Step 1: Identify the positive behavior you'd like to see more of. All you have to do is choose one or two behaviors that you want to see your child improve. Of course, you can respond in an affirming way to any positive behavior your child exhibits, but any trainer worth his salt knows that you can't teach everything at once. If your six-year-old child has a bad habit you'd like to change (such as arguing, throwing fits, or putting his cigarettes out on the couch*), then start with that. You can focus on another behavior later. Most parents I work with usually start with one (or both) of these areas:

- Responding respectfully to parents' requests (e.g., promptly obeying when asked to do something such as brush his teeth, do his homework, tar and shingle the roof, etc.)
- Responding respectfully when a situation doesn't go his or her way (e.g., being respectful and flexible when told that she can't have another cookie, needs to clean her room, can't move in with her boyfriend, etc.)

When you choose a specific behavior or two to focus on, you have a clear target to focus your words on, and it makes it easier for your kids to know what you are looking for.

Step 2: Watch carefully for that positive behavior to happen. There are so many things that demand a dad's attention: talk radio, March Madness, a sale on power washers at Home Depot. Rest assured, I would never ask you to give these things up. My point is simply that there are many things that vie for your attention every second, and in the midst of this battle, focusing on your children's positive behaviors often gets the shaft.

This is a problem. You become like a trainer who can't stay focused on his trainee. Picture a batting coach with his student at the batting cages. The batting student is concentrating hard on staying in the right stance and making contact with the balls flying at him, and he can't wait to get some feedback and guidance from the coach. But where's the coach? He is standing off to the side, laughing it up with the other coaches,

*An ashtray would be much better.

not even paying attention to his student. What kind of coach is that? It won't take long for the student to lose his motivation to work hard for this coach, because it is abundantly clear that the coach is not interested.

Jake's karate coach, Brian Mertel (an eight-time national champion and current member of the USANKF Senior Men's Karate Team), is a great coach and has become a good friend of our family. I can't tell you how many times I have seen Brian watch Jake compete in a karate match and then immediately point out very specific details that Jake did well or that he could improve on in his next match. Brian would draw Jake's attention to the twisting of his hips, the proper distance between Jake and his opponent before attacking, and various ways to set up his punches and kicks so that he would score. There was no doubt about it; Jake knew that Brian had been watching him very carefully.

In the same way, when you watch carefully for your child's positive behavior, you become aware of much more positive behavior than ever before. You see details and positive choices that you normally would have overlooked. This puts you in a position to respond with far greater frequency, which makes it easier for your child to see the connection between her positive behavior and your attention. Just like Brian watching Jake's every move at a karate match, a great dad will watch carefully for his child's positive behaviors and respond to every one he can.

Step 3: Immediately respond with a laser beam of positive attention. Here's the fun part. When your child shows the positive behaviors you are watching for, all you have to do is respond as quickly as you can with two things, and your "Pour It On" will have the knockout power of a Mike Tyson punch. Here they are:

1. *Physical touch.* This is dad power to the max. A high-five or a squeeze on the hand, arm, shoulder, or knee is all it takes. Light, affectionate physical touch creates a

warm, encouraging experience for your child and sends the unmistakable message "Dad loves me."

2. *A specific verbal reward.* This is the second part of the one-two punch. A specific verbal reward is simply a highly detailed description of your child's positive behavior given in a fun, positive way. Here are a few examples:

- "Holly, when I said you couldn't have a cookie just now, you said, 'That's okay,' and got an apple instead. That was an awesome way to handle it when you had to wait for something you wanted" (squeeze on the shoulder).

- "Billy, you just took your shoes off right away when your mom asked you to. Great job, buddy! Give me five!"

- "Theresa, you did an excellent job cleaning up your room. Look, your shoes are in the closet and your bed is so neat. It looks awesome, sweetie!" (gently touch her back).

Specific, affectionate, and positive. The combination of physical touch and a specific verbal reward is a secret weapon that is loaded with your positive attention, and your kids will love every blast.

How Often Should I Pour It On?

The real question is: How much positive behavior do you want? How respectful do you want your kids to be? Would you rather have good habits or bad? You may be thinking that you don't have that many Pour It On opportunities because you are at work all day. This is why the Pour It On Technique works even better when both mom and dad use it. However, wanting to give more Pour It Ons is not a valid excuse to quit your job. Nice try. You can have great dad impact with the time you currently have.

If your kids are behaving fairly well, I'd recommend that you aim for giving each child *three to five* Pour It Ons each day. If your children are not behaving well and you want to get things going in the right direction ASAP, then it's time to give them *five to ten* Pour It Ons each day. On some days you may have to look *really hard* to find those positive behaviors. But far more often than not, they're there. It's just a matter of you finding them.

What Happens Next?

Let me give you a fictional illustration. Let's say that little Johnny and Susie are playing in the family room, while you are in the kitchen, emptying the dishwasher.* Out of the corner of your eye, you see little Susie give Johnny an angry look and then wind up and punch him right in the face! You drop your silverware and immediately run over to Susie, give her a big squeeze, and say, "Susie, I just saw you hit little Johnny! And you know what . . . that was an awesome punch! You got him square in the jaw. Look at him, he's not even moving! And your form was great; the way you twisted your hips and followed through on your punch. Sweetie! You are going to be an Ultimate Fighting Champion someday!"

If you responded like that every time little Susie hit little Johnny, what would happen to Susie's hitting behavior? Would it go up or down?

It would go up.

What would happen to little Johnny?

He'd need a good medical plan.

The point here is that if the Pour It On Technique would make even a *negative* behavior increase, can you imagine what it will do for a positive behavior?

I can, because I've seen it happen hundreds of times. Challenging child behavior that was blasted to the outer orbit

---

*I said this is a fictional illustration.

94

of Naboo* by mom and dad simply using the Pour It On Technique. Your attention is an amazingly powerful secret weapon that can help your children realize how much fun it is (and how much dad and mom notice) when they are respectful. Or, to use a familiar phrase, how fun it is to be a gold nugget. Start today and see what happens. William Wallace would be proud of you. He might even give you a Man Card.

Key Points

1. Your words are powerful because they contain your attention.
2. To be most effective, a good trainer focuses on one or two target behaviors at a time.
3. High frequency means responding to the *majority* of times that your child behaves positively.
4. The combination of physical touch and a specific verbal reward will help your child experience how fun it is to be respectful.
5. Three to five Pour It Ons a day is good for maintenance. Use five to ten if you want to see the positive behavior really increase.

Getting to Work

1. The Bible has much to say about the power of our words. Read Proverbs 10:11, 20; 16:24; and 18:21. How do you like it when someone encourages you or points out something positive you have done? What impact does that encouragement have on your relationship with that person? What impact does it have on your behavior?
2. How do you think kids learn to be respectful? Do they just automatically know how to act respectfully and

*Do you know your Star Wars planets?

make good choices,* or do you think they need to be taught to be respectful and to make good choices?

3. What difference do you think the light, affectionate physical touch makes in the Pour It On Technique? How do you think your children will respond to receiving more affirming touches from you?

4. Here's a little practice. Name two specific positive behaviors you'd like to see each of your kids do more often. Come up with a specific verbal reward for each of these behaviors. How do you think your kids would feel if they heard these from you on a regular basis?

5. Time for an imagination exercise. Picture yourself giving around five Pour It Ons to each of your children every day for about two weeks. What difference do you think this would have on your children's behavior? Why don't you take it one step further and actually do a two-week Pour It On experiment? What do you have to lose?

_____

*And exactly *what* planet would those kids be from?

PART 3

How You Connect with Your Children

"Hello, My Name Is Dad"

I always enjoy it when Charles Barkley, aka the Round Mound of Rebound, appears on my television screen, whether he is providing his always colorful basketball commentary, is a guest on a late-night talk show, or has agreed to be the spokesman for some noble product that is vital to defeating Al Qaida and quelling terrorism around the world.* The NBA superstar and two-time Olympic gold medal–winning "Dream Team" member brings intelligence, a superb sense of humor, and a transparent love for the game each time he talks into the television camera. You might think that this young kid from Alabama has everything he ever dreamed of.

You'd be wrong.

In Sir Charles's book, *I May Be Wrong but I Doubt It,* he describes a painfully distant relationship with his father.

---

*Such as Nike shoes.

Barkley wrote that after a long time of trying to establish a connection with his dad, he just quit trying.

"I'm positive my old man never saw me play a basketball game in high school, never saw me play at Auburn. He never saw me play until I got in the NBA. He got interested in a relationship again when I became an NBA All-Star. . . . I started to visit him, spend some time with him. . . . But it seemed every time I went to LA all of our time was spent with him introducing me to all of his friends, his coworkers and associates. And it was clear what was going on there; he was just showing me off. I was his show pony."[1]

Learning to Spell

Barkley's father made a costly spelling mistake, one that each one of us can make. How do kids spell love? *Time.* As they get older, you may think they spell it *money* or *car.** But no, it always has been and always will be spelled *time.*

One morning several years ago I was lying in bed reading and praying while Lora was getting the kids ready for school. Jake was in first grade and Luke was in preschool. They were all dressed and ready to go and had some time left before they had to leave. However, instead of heading straight to the television to watch their brand-new Scooby-Doo videotape, Jake came upstairs, climbed on the bed, got under the covers with me, clothes and all, and laid his head on my chest. Sure enough, about fifteen seconds later, Luke climbed up the other side of the bed and lay down on my chest.

Delighted by this surprise intrusion, I rubbed each of their backs and we started to tell jokes, which had become one of our favorite things to do together. Having read this far, you know that my genetic heritage does not predispose me toward jokes of the highest quality. So our jokes that morning included the likes of: "What do you get when a cow gets

*Porsche, to be exact.

caught in an earthquake? A milkshake." But my boys, being of the same genetic heritage, didn't care as we laughed ourselves silly anyway.

That moment with my boys made me feel very special and very loved. Looking back, I can see two reasons why. First, even though the joke quality wasn't high, we were spending quality time together. Second, they *voluntarily* gave up Scooby-Doo to spend time with their dad. You must understand, they would forgo food and water to watch that videotape. The fact that this morning moment was 100 percent unsolicited was what impacted me the most. I had not called them into my room; they came all on their own.

As we told jokes on my bed that morning, it dawned on me that it works both ways. If I want my children to have that same feeling of being special and valued, then I need to spend quality time with them and be willing to give up my own high-priority activities simply because I would rather be with my children and family.

Even if it means missing Scooby-Doo.

Connect First

You may be wondering why I have devoted an entire section of this book to the topic of connecting with your kids. Jesus connected with his disciples and transformed their lives. For approximately three years, they were almost constantly together. Jesus spent *time* with his disciples in synagogues, walking from place to place throughout the countryside, and playing pick up sticks with leftover fish bones. In fact, his disciples became so connected with Jesus that history tells us that when given the choice, they chose to give up their lives rather than be unfaithful to their Lord.

Jesus's connection with his disciples opened the door for him to shape their lives for eternity. Similarly, as a great dad, you have a truckload of life-giving wisdom and guidance that God wants to transfer to your kids through you. We see this indicated in the opening chapter of Proverbs, where Solomon writes, "Listen, my son, to your father's instruction and do not forsake your mother's teaching. They will be a garland to grace your head and a chain to adorn your neck" (Prov. 1:8–9).

But how do you transfer that truckload of wisdom and guidance to your kids? The answer is that you connect first. Picture yourself on one side of a canyon and your kids on the other side. Unless you are related to Evel Knievel, you have to build a bridge over the canyon if you want to get across. In the same way, a great dad will connect with his kids by building a strong relationship bridge over which the wisdom and guidance can travel. I have seen many dads try to send their fully loaded "wisdom trucks" across the canyon without building a strong relationship bridge first, only to find that their trucks end up on the canyon floor. You have to connect before you can direct. And the stronger the connection, the more receptive your kids will be to your direction.*

Building a Strong Relationship Bridge

There's an old joke about a golfer who was walking around the fairway with four caddies following behind him. "Why so many caddies?" a friend asked. "It's my wife's idea," the golfer answered. "She thinks I should spend more time with the kids."[2] With that in mind, here are some strategies for making a strong and lasting "great dad" connection with your children.

1. *Maximize your together time.* Spending time together with your kids is absolutely necessary if you want to keep your connection strong. Why? Because your kids know that you are a grownup and can do pretty much whatever you want with your time, which explains why when not engaged in absolutely necessary dad tasks (i.e., sleeping), most dads can be found watching NASCAR. But out of all the things

---

*Yes, I write rap songs in my spare time.

102

you can choose from, you are choosing them. This makes your kids feel very special and important to you.

Here are a couple of the ways that I have stayed connected with my kids over the years. When my boys were younger, we loved to sit in their room and make up funny stories at bedtime. For example, one of our favorites was called *Fred the Head*. This was a story about a guy named Fred whose head kept falling off. While his body would feel around, trying to find its lost head, Fred's head would roll down a hill* into many adventures, such as getting mistaken for a soccer ball, or a bowling ball, or a cannonball in the circus, or a big red ball in the Shamu tank at SeaWorld, or, well, you get the idea.

While *Fred the Head* may or may not be your kind of story, my boys and I would laugh so hard that we'd all wet our pants. As the boys got older, we decided to stop wetting our pants and moved on to board games and backyard sports. Then came video games. I'll never forget how much fun we had playing the PlayStation Madden NFL football video game when we realized that you could make your players run into the referees and knock them over. Priceless.

As Jake and Luke have developed different interests, I have had plenty of opportunities to spend time individually with each of them as well. Our one-on-one times often center on their individual interests, such as practicing sports, working on music lessons, or manufacturing fake IDs. We have also read through a few good Christian books together, and we have sat at home (or at McDonald's) to discuss their thoughts on the latest chapter. A few of the books they enjoyed were *Leading from the Lockers* by John Maxwell, *The Case for Christ (Student Edition)* by Lee Strobel, *Geek-Proof Your Faith* by Greg Johnson and Michael Ross, and *A Young Man after God's Own Heart* by Jim George.

I encourage you to spend time with your kids in a variety of ways. You might even consider sitting down with your

*Funny, Fred always seemed to be standing by a hill.

kids and making a list together of fun things to do. Inside activities, outside activities, pretend play, board games, TV shows or movies, video games, outings, reading, building, talking, learning. Sometimes you'll just be having fun. Other times, you'll be using the activity as a backdrop to talk about important things happening in your child's life or to discuss a lesson from a recent experience or from a book you are reading together. Every time, however, you'll be making the most of your time together and building a strong relationship connection.

2. *Prioritize relationship over activity.* In *The Five Love Languages of Teenagers*, Gary Chapman points out that being in the same room with your kids, or even involved in an activity together, does not necessarily create a strong connection. For example, if a father and child are watching a football game together on television and the child gets the feeling that dad is more interested in the game than in his child, then, Chapman says, *togetherness* did not occur. Chapman shares the touching example of fifteen-year-old Clint, who said, "My father thinks he is doing me a favor when he takes me fishing. He calls it 'our buddy time' but we don't ever talk about us. Our conversations are about fishing and nature, but I don't care about fishing or nature. I wish I could talk to my father about my problems, but he doesn't seem interested in me."[3]

How I wish that Clint's dad had the twenty-five questions we discussed in chapter 1. Even though he was setting aside some one-on-one time, Clint's dad was apparently more connected with a bluegill than he was with his own son. How Clint's face would have lit up if his dad would have put his fishing pole down, focused his gaze on Clint, and asked him where his favorite vacation spot would be, who his closest friend is, or what he has been praying about recently.

No matter what the activity, a great dad will prioritize his relationship with his kids. Watching a movie, helping with homework, getting matching tattoos—any activity can be a relationship builder if you remember that it is another chance to connect with your child. Focusing your attention on your kids, engaging them in discussion, and making them feel loved and valued during these daily activities will strengthen your relationship by sending a "great dad" message: "I love you, I am interested in your life, and I am so thankful that you are my son/daughter."

3. *Utilize your body language.* One of the most powerful ways to send that "great dad" message during daily activities is through your body language. People will believe your nonverbal communication over your verbal communication every time. If you're a Monty Python fan, you'll remember the classic scene from *Monty Python and the Holy Grail* where the body collector pulls his cart, piled with dead bodies, into a small village (during the plague-stricken Middle Ages), shouting, "Bring out your dead!" A man walks toward the cart with an old man draped over his shoulders, while the old man protests, "I'm not dead yet." "I feel fine!" "I think I'll go for a walk." Unfortunately, the man is so old and frail that he cannot move. His verbal communication says he's alive and happy. His nonverbal communication says it's time to size him up for a coffin. The medieval body collector, seeing that if he doesn't take him now he'll just have to come back and pick him up in a week, solves his dilemma by matter-of-factly conking him on the head with a club, and then continues picking up bodies. Nonverbal wins.

To avoid getting conked on the head and put on the cart, here are some great body language relationship builders you can use to keep a strong connection with your kids every day:

- Hugs
- Kisses on the cheek and forehead
- Squeezes on the hands, shoulders, and knees
- High fives, fist bumps
- Warm smiles

- Looking directly at your kids when you are talking or listening to them
- Actually remaining awake during conversations

These simple but powerful nonverbal behaviors let your kids know that they are important to you. This makes them feel valued and loved, which means *you* are making them feel valued and loved. If you ever doubt the power of these relationship builders, just imagine what your relationship would be like without them.

Here's a little reminder from some of my friends (who are great dads) with daughters: while a daughter's privacy needs to always be respected, especially as she physically matures into a young woman, a daughter's need and desire to be connected with her dad doesn't diminish with time. This young woman is still daddy's little girl who wants to feel loved by and connected with her father. Buying her a bunny to hug won't cut it. So whether it is through hugs and goodnight kisses, holding hands occasionally while walking, or sitting close together while watching a movie, a great dad will find appropriate ways to stay physically connected with his daughter. Remember, you are modeling for your daughter how her future husband should treat her: affectionately, tenderly, but with respect and clear boundaries.

A Connection That Lasts

The lasting impact of a father-child connection was powerfully illustrated in the touching story of Debbie Moore and her father, Deryck Lawson, in Tim Russert's book *Wisdom of Our Fathers*. There were eight children in their family, two boys and six girls. Debbie and her sisters used to gang up on her father and comb his hair, put it in curlers, and paint his toenails. Enjoying his special time with his girls, Deryck just let them do it (talk about a *great* dad). That was forty years ago. About ten years ago, Deryck became terminally ill and the family had to make the heart-wrenching choice to take him off of life support. Debbie wrote that as the family sat at Deryck's hospital bedside during his final moments, "we six girls decided that it would be fitting for Dad to enter heaven with his toenails painted. Each of us painted a toe, and amid the tears, we all burst out laughing. The hospital staff must have thought we were crazy, but we knew something they didn't: Dad would have loved it."[4]

Those girls were connected with their dad to the very end. Why? Because their dad made it a point to connect with them from the very beginning. He built a relationship bridge and he kept it strong. By maximizing your together time, prioritizing relationship over activity, and utilizing your body language, you can start to connect with your children in a way that will open them up to the life-giving wisdom and guidance that God wants them to receive from you. They may not remember every word you've said *to* them, but they will remember the *time* you've spent *with* them. That's the power of the great dad that God wants to turn you into. And if you're not sure how important being connected with you is to your kids, just ask Charles Barkley.

Key Points

1. You connect with your kids by spending quality *time* with them.
2. You have to build a strong relationship bridge with your kids *before* God can transfer his wisdom and guidance over it.
3. Togetherness occurs when your child feels more important to you than the activity you are doing together.
4. Your body language is a powerful way to connect with your kids every day.
5. Your kids won't remember all the words you've said *to* them, but they will remember the *time* you've spent *with* them.

Getting to Work

1. Read Proverbs 1:8–9; 6:20–23. What kind of wisdom does God want to transfer through you to your children?
2. In order for that transfer of wisdom to take place, why is it so important to build a strong relationship bridge with your kids? How connected are you with each of your kids right now? Are any obstacles getting in the way of your connection?
3. Spending time with your kids and family is connection step number one. How much time do you spend with your kids, individually or as a family? What activities do you usually do with your kids? Are there any activities you want to add that will create a better balance of opportunities for fun, learning, and talking together?
4. List one activity that each of your children enjoy. Name two ways that, while doing that activity together, you can let your child know that you are more interested in him or her than in that activity.
5. Of the nonverbal relationship builders listed on pages 105–6, name two that you regularly do with your kids. What is one nonverbal behavior you can improve at that will make your relationship connection stronger?

Connect through Respect

Although he could be off-color at times, Rodney Dangerfield was one of my all-time favorite stand-up comics. His classic white shirt and red tie, along with his favorite line, "I don't get no respect," made him famous for his self-effacing one-liners. As a child psychologist, I have a soft spot in my heart for Rodney because according to his aptly titled little book, *I Don't Get No Respect*, it sounds like he had a rough childhood. Listen to his own words:

- When I was a baby they bought me a carriage with no brakes.
- Once I had a fever . . . they put a thermometer in my mouth and my old man said, "All right, kid, bite hard."
- One time I asked my old man if I could go ice skating on the lake . . . he told me to wait till it got warmer.[1]

Take it from me, experiences like these can do a number on your self-esteem, even more than losing to a group of nine-year-olds in a Pinewood Derby race. Poor guy, even as a kid he got no respect.

Usually when the topic of respect comes up in my office, the issue is about the kids learning to be respectful to their parents. In this chapter, however, we're going to flip it around and talk about how dads can jump-start their father-child connection by being respectful to their kids.

The One-Thousand-Dollar Bill

Ten-year-old Michael and his eight-year-old sister, Beth, were sitting on my big blue couch beside their mother. Mrs. Norris wanted us to talk about the topic of respect. To start our session, I took my pad of legal-sized paper and drew a one-thousand-dollar bill. Then I carefully folded around the edges of my counterfeit bill and tore away the excess paper until my bill was about the size of a regular dollar bill.

"This is a one-thousand-dollar bill," I said. Then, without another word, I crumpled it up and shoved it in my mouth. Now I had their full attention. After chewing on it for a while, I spit it onto the carpet and stepped on it, grinding it into the floor with my shoe. Then I stomped on it a few times for good measure. By this time, both kids had one eye glued on me and the other on the door, wondering if they should make a break for it while they still had a chance. I'm sure Mrs. Norris was wondering if it was too late to get a refund.*

I picked up the thousand-dollar bill, unwrinkled it, and showed it to the family. "Okay, guys," I asked, "if this was a real thousand-dollar bill, is this how I should treat it?"

"No," both kids answered.

"Why not?"

*In case you plan to have me work with your kids in the future, yes, it was too late.

110

"Because you'd wreck it," Michael stated.

"It's already ripped," Beth added, "and it's all sticky."

"So what?" I continued. "Does it matter?"

They thought for a second. "It's a thousand-dollar bill," Michael said. "You don't want to waste it."

"So you think I should take care of it?" I asked.

"Yeah," they both nodded.

"I think you're right," I said with a smile. "But *why* should I take care of it?"

Beth answered, "'Cause it's worth a lot of money."

"Would you both agree that a thousand-dollar bill is valuable?" I asked, starting to move us closer to the main point of our little demonstration.

"Yes," they both replied.

"And how should you treat something that is valuable?" I asked. "Should you crumple it up, spit on it, roll it in the dirt, stomp on it, or throw it in the garbage can?"

"No," they instinctively responded.

"That's right," I said, getting ready to lower the boom. "If you have something valuable, you take good care of it. You look after it. You keep it in a safe place. You protect it. In other words, you treat it with a great deal of (dramatic pause) . . . ?"

The lightbulb went on for both of them at the same time as they completed my sentence in unison: "Respect."

There Is No Other Way

I recently had a mother tell me how disrespectful her son is to her and how difficult that makes it for her to want to spend time with him. While part of her longs for a close connection with her son, the other part of her feels like washing his mouth out with twenty tons of industrial-strength soap.*

*I am not in favor of washing a child's mouth out with twenty tons of industrial-strength soap. Ten tons should work just fine.

111

This is exactly the situation we want to avoid: a relationship connection that is damaged because one of the persons in that relationship is treating the other disrespectfully. While the person behaving disrespectfully in your family will be your child on occasion, we *never* want it to be you. This mom has her work cut out for her, to be sure, but one of the things she must do is treat her son in a respectful way.

"What?" you gasp in disbelief. "Treat him respectfully even if he treats her disrespectfully?"

Especially *because* he is treating her disrespectfully. Your child will learn to be respectful during his difficult moments by seeing how his parents are respectful during their difficult moments. Part of a great dad's job is to show his kids how to do it *right*. They already know how to do it wrong, so they don't need your help in that department. In Luke 6:31, Jesus commands us to: "Do to others as you would have them do to you." If we would have our children learn to treat others respectfully, then we must treat them respectfully, when it is easy and when it is hard. When we feel like it and when we don't.

Respectful behavior has relationship-connecting power. This is because people only open the relationship connection door to those who treat them in a respectful way. You wouldn't open your front door to someone who walks in and kicks you in the shin. At least not twice. And neither will your child. The reason is simple. When a dad treats his kids with respect, he is communicating to them that they are special and valuable to him. That he will protect and look after them. That they are even more valuable to him than a thousand-dollar bill.

Now let me be clear: treating your kids respectfully does not mean you cater to their every whim. It simply means that your daily interactions with them send what we'll call the respect message: "As my son/daughter, you (and other family members) are the most important people in my life. I will always love and protect you as God's precious handiwork. I

112

will do my best to treat you with the same respect and value that I want you to treat others with."

The Family Respect Rule

So how does a great dad get the respect train rolling? In my book *Keep the Siblings, Lose the Rivalry*,[2] I introduce something I like to call the Family Respect Rule. It reads like this:

Everyone in our family needs to treat everyone else in our family respectfully. All the time.

Simple and to the point. Now, let's see if you're smarter than a fifth grader. Here is a little Family Respect Rule quiz. First question: *To whom* does the Family Respect Rule apply? Answer: Everyone. For our purposes in this chapter, everyone starts with dad. In fact, your kids are watching you to see how important the Family Respect Rule really is and how seriously they should follow it.

Second question: *When* does the Family Respect Rule apply? Answer: All the time. The Family Respect Rule doesn't end with "as long as your child is being really, really nice." When is it okay to draw a mustache on the *Mona Lisa*? Never, though I admit it would be *slightly* funny.* To put it in dad terminology, this means that there is *never* a time when it is okay for *you* to be disrespectful to someone in your family with your words or actions. But you can draw a mustache on them.

Third question: What is the *basis* for the Family Respect Rule? Answer: Everyone in your family was created by whom? God. Everyone in your family is of incredible value to whom? God. Everyone in your family is worth far more than our thousand-dollar bill. As Jesus said, "Are not two sparrows

*But highly illegal, and I do not recommend it.

sold for a penny? Yet not one of them will fall to the ground apart from the will of your Father. And even the very hairs of your head are all numbered. So don't be afraid; you are worth more than many sparrows" (Matt. 10:29–31).

Your children are God's precious gold nuggets that he has entrusted into your care. Your child's value doesn't diminish when he acts disrespectfully. He simply becomes God's gold nugget who is making a very bad choice at that moment. But he is still as precious and important, and your job is still the same: to help your child learn the right lessons in the right way. A respectful way.

A Father Only Builds

In *Bringing Up Boys*, psychologist James Dobson shares that General Douglas MacArthur, the World War II military legend, is one of his heroes. In explaining why he holds MacArthur in such high esteem, Dobson shares a quote from a speech MacArthur gave in 1942 after receiving an award for being a good father: "Nothing has touched me more deeply than [this honor given to me] by the National Father's Day committee," MacArthur said. "By profession, I am a soldier and take great pride in that fact. But I am prouder, infinitely prouder, to be a father. A soldier destroys in order to build. The father only builds, never destroys. The one has the potentialities of death, the other embodies creation and life. And while the hordes of death are mighty, the battalions of life are mightier still. It is my hope that my son, when I am gone, will remember me not from the battle, but in the home."[3]

I love the line "the father only builds, never destroys." Disrespectful behavior destroys relationship connections, whether it is between kids, friends, marriage partners, or a father and a child. Respectful behavior builds them. Remember the relationship bridge we talked about in chapter 9? You want to protect that bridge. You want to build it even stronger than it is. That bridge is the only way you will get wisdom, guidance, and influence from your side of the canyon to your child's side. You never want to hurt or damage the bridge. You sure don't want to destroy it.

So how do you build the bridge and keep your relationship connection strong? All you have to do is treat your kids the same way you treat anything else of great value to you. Think of an object you own that is very special or important to you. Your golf clubs. The television remote control. Your Bosch 36-volt hammer power drill with a unibody powertrain that can withstand repeated drops from the roof of a one-story building.* How do you treat this object? I bet you take care of it. You make sure not to damage it, even accidentally. You might have a nice case for it. You keep it maintained and polished. You protect it by not letting just anyone use it. As I said earlier, you treat it with respect.

Now, take that concept and apply it to your kids. No, that doesn't mean you put them in a case. You treat your kids respectfully by remembering how valuable they are to you. And to God. You value their feelings and their ideas. You give your kids a chance to tell you how they think and feel at any time (as long as they do it respectfully). You are thankful every time your kids open up and share something personal with you. You protect them. You make sure you don't hurt them, physically or emotionally, even by accident. You watch out for damaging communication hazards. You make sure to spend plenty of time with them. You use lots of warm physical touch. You smile at them. You tell them you love them. You discipline them in a way that communicates your desire for them to learn an important lesson, not in a way that vents your anger.

A child who is treated this way by his dad will *want* to be connected with that dad. Children from other continents will want to be connected with that dad. That dad's respectful behavior has opened the door to a relationship connection

---

*Make ape-like grunting noise here.

that can last a lifetime. He has built the bridge and is keeping it strong. Jesus reminded us that we are worth more than many sparrows to the Father. I know that your children are worth more than many sparrows to you. Make sure they know it too.

Key Points

1. When something is valuable, you treat it with respect.
2. Treating your children respectfully communicates that they are valuable and important to you.
3. The Family Respect Rule applies to everyone in your family, but it starts with dad.
4. A great dad only builds relationship connections; he never destroys them.
5. A father who treats his children with value and respect will have children who *want* to be connected with him.

Getting to Work

1. What do you think of the thousand-dollar bill illustration? How would you summarize the main point of that lesson? Do you think you would ever use this illustration with your kids?
2. Read Ephesians 2:10 and Luke 6:31. These verses tell us that your children are God's workmanship that you are to treat in the same way you would like to be treated. With these verses in mind, why is it important for a dad to treat his children with respect? What lessons does this teach his kids? What lessons do his kids learn if he *doesn't* treat them with respect?
3. Read the Family Respect Rule out loud. Using this rule as your measuring stick, give yourself a 1 to 10 score for how respectfully you treat your kids. Why did you give yourself this score? Do you think your kids would give you the same score?

4. What is your biggest obstacle to treating your kids with respect? What impact do you think your disrespectful behavior has on your relationship with your kids? Name one step you can take to improve in this area.
5. Douglas MacArthur stated, "The father only builds, never destroys." Name three things you will do this week to build your relationship with each of your kids.

Listen and Learn

They were worn and weary, yet Frodo and Sam continued on their journey to Mordor, dodging foul-smelling Orcs at every turn and with the "We hates these Hobbitses" Gollum as their guide. Not exactly a Bahamas pleasure cruise. Finding the Black Gate into Mordor closed for visitors (it was the off-season), they had to take the back way in, which meant climbing the rather inhospitable stairs of Cirith Ungol, which were cut into the Mountains of Shadow on the western border of Mordor.

All along the journey, Sam's distrust of Gollum's motives had been growing. Blinded by the power of the ring, Frodo felt a strange kinship to Gollum, whose life had been severely twisted and strangely prolonged by the ring* when it had been in his possession. Sam, of course, was correct in his distrust of Gollum, whose plan was to lead Frodo to Shelob, the giant

---

*Not to mention incurring a bad case of hair loss and serious gingivitis.

spider who lived at the top of the mountain and who just loved to have little Hobbitses drop in for dinner.

The final straw came in the early hours of the morning, when Gollum stole the remaining lembas bread that Frodo and Sam had been surviving on, threw it over the mountainside, and then blamed it on Sam. Sam tried to tell Frodo that he had been framed, but the lembas bread crumbs that Gollum had secretly sprinkled on Sam's shirt were all the proof Frodo needed to conclude that Sam's carbohydrate addiction could no longer be tolerated. As Frodo sent Sam home, a smirking Gollum could almost feel the imprint of the ring in his hand, as he was planning to pry it out of Frodo's soon-to-be paralyzed body. A tearful Sam tried to tell Frodo that he was making a huge mistake.

But Frodo wasn't listening.

Unload the Truck

If we were to ask Frodo if he wished he had done a better job of listening to Sam instead of his little finger-biting friend Gollum,* I suspect his answer would be a resounding, "*Yes! What, do you think I enjoyed being stung by a five-hundred-pound spider?*" As the result of his failure to listen to his good friend, Frodo placed their entire mission, the lives of every man and Hobbit in Middle Earth, and the entire Lord of the Rings franchise in serious jeopardy.

Being a good listener is really just a logical extension of the Family Respect Rule we discussed in chapter 10. If your children are valuable, then their thoughts, opinions, and feelings are valuable. And what do you do with valuable thoughts, opinions, and feelings? You listen to them.

When kids have something to say, they are often like a dump truck. However, I don't mean to imply that they are filled with dirt or rotten garbage; let's say that their truck is

---

*Thanks to whom Frodo's chances of ever playing in the NBA are now over.

filled with something very valuable, like diamonds. The point is, simply, that their truck is full. There is no room for any more material. You can pile it on all you'd like, but it will just fall off the top and make a mess on the carpet.

What is one to do in this situation? Well, the obvious step, if you were a city employee, would be to take a thirty-minute break, followed by a succession of additional thirty-minute breaks, until it is time to go home. However, seeing as we don't work for the city, the logical step for a great dad would be to unload the truck. That is what listening does. It allows your kids to unload the cargo they have been storing up.

What kind of valuable cargo are we talking about? Your child's thoughts and feelings. The little stuff and the big stuff.* The new friend she met at school. The cool LEGO Star Wars ship that he just put together. That the popular girl made fun of her new haircut. How he thinks it is unfair that his sister gets to stay up later than he does. How stressed out she is about her grades. The new girl he is starting to have feelings for. How much she is looking forward to the slumber party this weekend. The fact that his sister keeps bossing him around when you and mom are out of earshot.

A truck full of valuable diamonds. Once the truck is unloaded, it will be much easier for your child to listen to and benefit from your perspective and guidance. But the first step is to unload the truck.

How to Be a Great Listener

If you want to be a great dad, then becoming a great listener is part of the package. Here are a few great dad listening tips to get you started:

1. *Listen first, talk second.* Comedian Ronnie Shakes joked that after twelve years of therapy, his psychiatrist said something that brought tears to his eyes: "*No hablo ingles.*"[1]

*Clever concept tie-in from chapter 5.

Proverbs 18:13 puts it this way: "He who answers before listening—that is his folly and his shame."

Now, I've had enough folly and shame for ten lifetimes, so I don't need to add any more by making the mistake of answering before listening. The secret to this tip is to remember to let your child unload the truck first. Now, I don't mean to let her *start* unloading the truck and then jump in. Let her actually *finish* unloading the truck. Yes, the whole truck. Until she tells you she's done. Duct tape might be helpful here (for you, not your child).

Chances are that your child may not be expecting you to let her unload the truck, so you will need to let her know that this is what you want her to do. Here are some catchy ways of letting your kids know that you're ready to listen:

- "Okay, Susie, tell me how you feel about it."
- "John, I'd really like to hear your opinion about this."
- "All right, Chloe, before I say anything, I'd like you to have a chance to tell me what happened."
- "Tell me what you mean."
- "Katie, I'd love to hear more about what you think."
- "I'm not sure I understand what you mean. Can you explain it to me?"
- "What happened next?"
- "Is there anything else I need to know?"

Each of these statements lets your kids know that you *want* to hear what they have to say. This immediately makes them feel valuable, like you are really interested in what they are going to say. Another wonderful thing happens as well. Your child's defensiveness drops like a rock. You no longer have two people fighting for the microphone at the karaoke bar. You have handed your child the mike and taken a seat. Now the communication can begin.

2. *Listen to understand.* Listening doesn't mean agreeing with everything your child says. Good thing too, or you'd be having Fruit Roll-Ups for breakfast every morning. It just means making a genuine effort to understand what they think or how they feel. It is being willing to put yourself in their shoes for a couple minutes and look at the situation from their perspective.

Now, this type of listening is not a natural thing for me to do. I like the kind of discussion where I express my ideas and you say, "Those are the greatest ideas I have ever heard. Possibly the greatest ideas in the history of the earth." End of discussion. Unfortunately, the rest of my family doesn't go along with that. That's not "how they roll," as my sons would say in their hip, twenty-first-century high school lingo. So I am learning how to listen to Lora and to my boys. And the funny thing is, I have never once been sorry that I did.

Proverbs 14:8 reminds us that "The wisdom of the prudent is to give thought to their ways." I have found that taking the time to understand my sons' views on any topic we are discussing helps me to "give thought to my ways" so that I can make a better decision as a father. Listening to them gives me insight into how my boys are thinking and (although it might be scary) *what* they are thinking. I get a glimpse into their decision-making process and their problem-solving skills. It helps me to look at a certain situation from a different perspective and realize that it may be much more important to them than I had thought. It points out (on rare occasions, and I do mean *rare*) that I may have overlooked a few important facts that my boys have not made the mistake of overlooking. At times I have been impressed with the perspective and maturity that my sons have demonstrated when I have taken the time to listen to them. Other times I have seen mistakes and gaps in their thinking that have given me clues for how to help them think through a situation from a logical or biblical viewpoint more completely.

All of this has been possible *only* because I am learning to listen with the goal of truly understanding how they think and feel. Even better, listening to understand strengthens our relationship connection because I'm treating them (and what they think) with respect. I'm the dad; I'll have plenty of time to say what I think later. But first I want to listen to my boys the way I want them to listen to me.

3. *Listen actively.* Just as your body language is a powerful relationship connecting tool (as we discussed in chapter 9), it is also the main way your kids will know you are listening to them. Listening actively just means letting your kids know that you're not yet in full REM sleep while they're talking to you, which is the typical setting for most dad activities such as business meetings, freeway driving, and any type of shopping that is not for power tools.

Here are a few body language clues that will show your kids if you are listening or not:

Active listening	Passive listening
Eyes intently focused on them	Eyes slowly drift back into your head until only the whites are showing
Body squarely facing them	Body twitching, as if in a deep sleep
Mouth asking active listening questions	Drooling
Hands resting casually at your side	Secretly checking your Blackberry for sports scores

Summary statements are another great way to let your kids know you are listening. As you might guess from its clever name, a summary statement briefly summarizes what your child has communicated and demonstrates that you actually *were* listening carefully to what she said. When you summarize, all you have to do is zero in on the main points and feelings she stated or implied, like this:

Okay, Olivia, let's see if I've got this right. You would like a later bedtime because several of your friends get to stay up later than you, and you feel confused and maybe even frustrated about why we don't let you stay up later. Is that close?

With that kind of a summary, how can Olivia feel misunderstood? You have identified the main issues she is concerned about and have shown her that you are making your best dad effort to understand how she feels about them. The discussion will continue on from there, with Olivia answering her father, her father sharing his thoughts on her bedtime, Olivia responding, and so on. It will be like a friendly game of catch instead of a deadly game of dodgeball. And each time Olivia talks, she can be sure of one thing: her dad is listening.

When you let your kids unload their trucks by listening first, listening to understand, and listening actively, your discussions will be more productive than ever before, and you will learn more about what your kids think and feel than you ever thought you could. Best of all, your listening will make your children feel like a valuable part of your family and will strengthen your relationship connection. Thanks to you, Middle Earth will live to see another day.

Key Points

1. Children have a natural desire to be known and understood by their parents.
2. Listening is nothing more than letting your child unload his or her truck.
3. Being willing to listen first communicates that you are really interested in your child's thoughts and feelings and reduces his or her defensiveness.
4. Listening to understand will give you a firsthand view of your child's decision-making process and will help you "give thought to your ways" when it is time to respond.
5. Listening actively with your body language and summary statements will show your child that you are really

trying to understand the situation from his or her perspective and will make you a dad your kids will want to talk to.

Getting to Work

1. Read Proverbs 10:19; 18:13; and James 1:19. Why does the Bible say it is important to be a good listener? Why is listening such an important part of staying connected with your kids?
2. How does it help you to think of your kids' thoughts and feelings as a truck full of valuable diamonds?
3. How does listening first promote effective communication with your kids? Have you noticed the difference in your child's receptiveness when you listen first as opposed to when you talk first?
4. Can you remember a time when you felt really listened to? What impact did that have on your relationship with the person who made you feel understood? Name one or two benefits of listening with the purpose of really understanding your child's thoughts and feelings.
5. Which active listening steps will communicate to your kids that you really are interested in what they have to say? Choose two (e.g., eyes focused on them, summary statements) and put them to work whenever you talk to your kids this week. At the end of the week, tell your kids you have been working on being a good listener and ask them if they have felt listened to (note: make sure you listen to their answer). Tell them that you are going to keep on working at being a good listener and that you welcome their feedback any time.

Connect as a Family

It was a cool but sunny Saturday morning in August as Lora, Jake, and I sat on the sidelines of the practice football field at Geneva High School and watched Luke play in the freshman football scrimmage, one week before their first game. All the boys played hard and had a good time. After the game, however, the fun really began.

For starters, the freshman players had to gather on the field in front of the varsity football team and sing the Geneva fight song. Whenever the varsity players detected the slightest hint of a lack of enthusiasm, they began to mercilessly boo the freshmen, who then had to repeat the fight song from the beginning. This happened several times, with the varsity players greatly enjoying the booing and the observing parents getting a kick out of the whole process.

Luckily for all of us, it didn't take more than five times through the fight song for the freshman team to get the message that the varsity players and coaches expected them to sing every syllable of their school fight song with pride. When the freshmen finally sang the fight song with full chest-thumping Geneva gusto to the level that pleased the varsity players, the varsity team walked over to the freshman team and joined in the last half of the song, creating a testosterone-enhanced choir of sorts and signaling that the freshmen had passed the test.

But they were not done yet. The freshmen were then instructed to sit down on the grass while the varsity players walked over to a table filled with watermelon slices and then served the slices to the freshmen. After the freshmen had eaten their watermelon, the varsity players sat down and the freshmen then served them watermelon slices. The freshmen then had to clean up the watermelon rinds and, for a final touch, carry the varsity players' helmets and shoulder pads back to the locker room.*

The coaches told us that this creative team-building exercise was a Geneva football tradition and that it was designed to build a sense of football family. Judging by what I saw on the players' faces that morning, I think it worked.

Creating a Family Culture

In his book *The Seven Habits of Highly Effective Families*, Stephen Covey coined the term "family culture." I have always loved that phrase, because it implies that your family can have its own culture no matter what those around you do. It's as if your family is its own little island with its own governing body. You have interaction with the other islands around you, so you know what they are doing, but you can make your own decisions for your island.

Before you get carried away with the island metaphor and start thinking that you can vote people off the island any time you want, let's get back to Covey's original idea. Covey defines a family culture as "the climate, character, spirit, feel-

---

*A few kids had to actually carry a varsity *player*.

ing, and atmosphere of the home and family."[1] I remember thinking to myself when my kids were young, "I can't control what other families do, but this is *my* family, and I want to do everything I can to create a great family culture." Then I fell back to sleep.

Lora and I decided back then that we would intentionally spend time together as a family, create memories, and develop "family habits" that would add to a positive family culture instead of detract from it. Out of all our efforts to create a close family, one of our decisions has had more impact than any other,* and I'd like to share it with you now.

A Regular Family Time

I can't tell you how grateful I am that we started having family times when our kids were roughly kindergarten age. I don't think it would have done as much good if we would have waited until they were in college. When I say regular, I mean weekly. We found that when our kids were young, we pretty much controlled their social schedule, so making a weekly family time happen was fairly easy to do. As our boys have gotten older, we have spread our family times out, but we still build them into our calendar on a regular basis.

Something powerful is communicated when you have a *regular* family time. As a psychologist I have learned that if anything happens to a person regularly, it is either biological or intentional. For instance, when a dad regularly forgets the passage of time whenever his favorite football team is playing, any physician will tell you this is clearly *biological*, and the dad cannot be held accountable for this genetically programmed lapse of awareness of the world around him. On the other hand, when a dad regularly decides to put his underwear in the laundry hamper,† this is clearly *intentional*,

*Even more than introducing our boys to the marvel of antiperspirant.
†That is, within a five-foot radius.

and the dad should receive full credit for his selfless effort to create an odorless and bacteria-free environment for his family.

In the same way, your children know that when you choose to have a *regular* family time, it is either biological or intentional. They are pretty sure it is not biological because there is no football involved. So it must be intentional. And when you intentionally choose to do something on a regular basis, then that something must be pretty important to you. In this case, that something is your family time. And your family usually includes your kids. Which means your kids must be pretty important to you.

That's the message that regular sends: *important.* Your regular family time communicates to your kids, louder than any words could ever do, "Our family is important to us. We're going to invest time into it, value it, learn how to follow God together, talk about important things, and have a great time doing it. This is not a practice; this is the real thing. The game is on. And we're going to do our best to do it right!"

The Two Components

Over the years, Lora and I have discovered that our family times worked best when we focused on two things: having fun together and bonding/learning together. So, based on our experience, here are the two components that I believe are essential to an effective family time:

1. *A fun activity.* This part is not rocket science. Kids like to have fun, and since we want them to like the family times, inserting some fun sounds like a reasonable thing to do. Plus, it helps make for some great family bonding and memories. A couple years ago we decided to make a gingerbread house together at Christmastime. It sounded like a fun and fairly simple family time activity. However, as we started our construction project, we quickly realized that we had seriously underestimated the skill that was apparently needed to make

a gingerbread house. Or at least to make one that stood up straight. Oh yes, and that had a roof.

As we looked in dismay at our slanted house with its roof that was more horizontal than diagonal and looked like it would cave in at any moment, we joked that it looked like the type of jail you might see in an old western movie. Then it hit us: let's make it into a jail! With our imaginations rejuvenated, we fashioned our house into a run-down, old-style jail, complete with a porcelain toilet made out of white frosting (I know they didn't have porcelain toilets back in those days, but we didn't care). Except for the toilet, it looked like it came right out of *Butch Cassidy and the Sundance Kid*. We even made a gingerbread prisoner. It wasn't much to look at, but it was a fun bonding time that resulted in a lot of laughter, and it was an experience that we'll all remember for a long time. We took pictures to make sure we do.

Building gingerbread jails may not be your cup of tea, so how you have fun with your family will be up to you. I just wanted to emphasize that fun makes a lasting impression. Sometimes we have started our family time with a fun activity, and other times we have ended it with a fun activity. Our fun activities have included the typical assortment, such as playing an age-appropriate board game, going to the park, taking a walk, bowling, getting some ice cream, baking and decorating cookies, playing miniature golf, going to the zoo, canoeing, watching a movie, and so on. Once we're done with our fun activity, then it is time for the real action to begin.

2. *Meaningful discussion.* While I love everything about family times, this is my favorite part. I love talking together about things that are important and listening to our kids tell us about what is happening in their lives. While the three categories of meaningful discussion for many dads include (1) their current fantasy sports team, (2) their past fantasy sports teams, and (3) who they *wish* they had on their fantasy sports team, our family time discussions have tended to fall into three different categories.

The first is *family devotions*. For us, this has usually involved reading a chapter from a devotional book and talking about it together. While there are many good books for this purpose, a few of the books we have used include *Little Visits for Families* by Allan Hart Jahsmann and Martin Simon; *The Purpose-Driven Life* by Rick Warren; and *The Day I Met God* by Karen Covell, Jim Covell, and Victorya Michaels Rogers. These books have been great resources in helping us to launch a discussion on a biblical topic and talk together about how to apply the lesson to our lives.

The second way that we have used our meaningful discussion time has been to talk about *individual/family issues*—current issues that were going on in the lives of our kids or our family. We have talked about school, grades, issues with peers, lessons God has been teaching us, and recent struggles or challenges our family has faced. I have particularly enjoyed our check-ins on how we are doing at treating each other respectfully or how well we are communicating together.

Recently, we decided to create a family mission statement, as Stephen Covey talks about in *The Seven Habits of Highly Effective Families*. Even though our boys were older, we decided it is better late than never. We read the "Family Mission Statement" chapter from Covey's book and got to work. I loved our discussions and the sense of tangible family commitment that came from those discussions. We thought long and hard about each of the statements we included. Luke volunteered to take our finished family mission statement and graphically design it on a sheet of paper to frame and place in a strategic location. Here it is:

We will be a family that *always*:

• Loves and obeys God	• Protects each other
• Listens to each other's feedback	• Treats each other respectfully
• Speaks the truth to each other in a loving way	• Has fun together

• Is quick to apologize and forgive   • Prays together
• Helps each other grow

Do you see why I love family times? Even as my boys go off to college and afterward, we will use this family mission statement to remind us of the kind of family we want to always be.

The third and final way we have used our meaningful discussions has been to work on what I call *living together skills*. These are the skills that anyone needs if they are going to live together successfully with any other human being. In my book *Keep the Siblings, Lose the Rivalry*,* I include several Family Time Discussion Guides that are focused on helping kids learn valuable living together skills such as these:

- The Family Respect Rule
- How to communicate respectfully
- Responding to sibling aggravation
- Being flexible
- Suggesting a solution
- Forgiving each other

We all loved the fun object lesson or activity that came with each family time, while the discussion questions and role-playing helped us to practice applying these important skills to urgent and possibly life-threatening family situations (such as when one boy has accidentally placed ⅜ of an inch of his big toe into the other boy's room without asking permission). We actually used several of the Family Time Discussion Guides more than once, to help us review skills when we thought we needed a brush-up.

---

*This is where I again take any chance I can to shamelessly promote my extremely helpful books.

Finally, we always close our family time by praying together. Sometimes one of us closes in prayer. Other times we share our prayer requests and then go around in a circle, praying for the person on our left. It is a wonderful thing to hear your children praying for each other, especially when you keep in mind the other types of words they *could* be using.

The Result

I don't know what type of results you have gotten from your family times, if you have done them before. I can only tell you that they have made a huge difference in our family. We have talked about the kind of family we want to be, have practiced the skills we need to become that family, and have had a lot of fun doing it. I encourage you to invest the time to create a warm, loving family culture, just as Luke's football coaches worked to create a close-knit team. A regular family time will be a big part of what makes that happen. And if you run out of ideas for fun activities, you can always have them sing the Geneva fight song.[2]

Key Points

1. You (and your wife) are responsible for creating your own family culture.
2. Having a *regular* family time shows your kids how important they are to you.
3. Including a fun activity in your family times makes them enjoyable and memorable.
4. Your meaningful discussions can focus on family devotions, individual/family issues, and living together skills.
5. Praying together is a wonderful way to connect and support each other as a family as you bring each other's needs before God.

Getting to Work

1. Using Covey's definition of a family culture, how would you describe your current family culture? What is something about your current family culture that you like and something you'd like to improve?
2. Do you have a regular family time? How has it impacted your family? If you have not had a regular family time, what has prevented you?
3. Read Deuteronomy 6:5–9. How will having a regular family time help you teach God's commands to your children in a fun and practical way?
4. List three fun activities you can do with your family as part of your family time.
5. Of the three categories of meaningful discussion (e.g., family devotions, individual/family issues, living together skills), which will help your family the most right now? Why did you choose this category? If you are married, discuss this chapter with your wife this week and make a plan to begin family times right away.

PART 4

Your Hands

How You Act toward Your Children

Be a Coach

James Robert Kennedy was a mentally handicapped young man whose life was changed forever by a coach. Not even his own coach, because he was not on any team. He lived with his mother and wandered around the small town of Anderson, South Carolina, putting various items in his shopping cart. He earned the nickname of Radio because of the transistor radio he carried wherever he went. Through a series of events, Radio was befriended by Harold Jones, coach of the Hanna Hornets football team. Despite resistance from some in the community, Coach Jones let Radio spend time at the high school, allowed him to help with the football and basketball teams, and even taught him how to write his name.

The wonderfully inspirational movie *Radio* is based on this true story. In fact, as of this writing, Radio is sixty-two years old and remains a welcome fixture at T. L. Hanna High School, helping daily in the lunch room and hallways and assisting with the football team. He is beloved by the community of Anderson and is an amazing example of the difference a coach (and a community) can make. If you haven't seen the movie, I recommend it for your next family time.

Every Child Needs a Coach

Radio was fortunate to have a coach like Harold Jones—a coach who saw in him what no one else took the time to see and who loved him enough to bring it out of him. Your kids need a coach like that. That's why God gave them you.

Will Rogers once observed, "There are three kinds of men. The one that learns by reading. The few who learn by observation. The rest of them have to pee on the electric fence for themselves."[1] We'd like for your kids to have to electrify their private regions as few times as possible in this lifetime, and for that to happen, they need a coach. And guess what? The Bible happens to think so too. One of my favorite parenting verses tells us to "Train a child in the way he should go, and when he is old he will not turn from it" (Prov. 22:6). Not train as in choo-choo but train as in teach, guide, and instruct. Or in other words: coach.

When Luke began playing football in seventh grade, I encouraged him to give the quarterback position a try, because he had a naturally good arm. However, his middle school football team had one main coach with one main job: to teach *every* position. I don't know what they paid him, but it clearly wasn't enough; otherwise I don't think he would have shouted as much as he did. He was teaching the blockers how to block, the tackles how to tackle, the linebackers how to lineback, and so on. He had so many positions to teach that by game time, he was just happy if the quarterback threw the ball in the general direction of the field.

It wasn't until we took Luke to a quarterback coach that I realized there were actual skills for being a quarterback. Where to hold the ball. How to drop back with the right footwork. When to smile at the college recruiters. As Luke began to learn and practice these skills, he started to look like a quarterback. He already had the talent; he just needed someone to shape it.

Your kids already have lots of great stuff packed inside of them. They just need a coach to help bring it out. To teach them how to do it right. To work with them when they do it wrong. That's what a coach does, and that's what your kids need if they are going to succeed. They've got some mighty big opponents ahead. God is the owner of the team, and you're the coach. So, in the words of Hank Williams Jr.: Are you ready for some football?

Thinking Like a Coach

Notice that I said your kids need a coach, not a referee. A referee focuses on enforcing the rules and meting out penalties when those rules are broken. It's an important function to be sure, and a good coach knows how to play within the rules of the game. But a coach is so much more than a referee. A coach focuses on what he wants his players to *learn*. He spends hours in practice with his players, showing them how to perform their positions the *right* way, helping them to develop *good* habits, and teaching them *why* these good habits are so important.

This is an entirely different way of thinking about childhood behavior than most of us are used to. We are used to responding to our kids' behavior when it creates a problem. That is being a referee. A coach responds to the problem as well, but then makes a note of it and starts to work on fixing it at the next practice. That is when he becomes a coach. *He turns the problem situation into a skill that can be taught and a lesson that can be learned.*

In the same way, every negative behavior our kids do and every problem they face can be turned into a positive skill or lesson. The lesson of talking respectfully to their parents. The skill of being flexible when something doesn't go their way.

The lesson of waiting until an older brother is *fully* asleep before trying to paint his toenails red. The lessons are there, waiting to be taught. All your kids need is a coach.

Your Coaching Playbook

A boy turned in a poem to his teacher. After reading it his teacher told him, "Justin, your poem is the worst in the class. It's not only ungrammatical, it's rude and in bad taste. I'm going to send your father a note about it." Justin replied, "I don't think that would help, Ma'am. He wrote it."[2]

Justin's dad didn't know much about writing poems, and some of you may be thinking, *I don't know much about coaching.* No problem. There are two basic coaching strategies you can use to turn any problem situation into a positive skill or lesson.

1. *Identify the area of need.* Two things are always happening with your kids: they are always thinking and responding.* You can use these two areas to pinpoint where your child needs help in order to handle things better the next time around.

a. *Thinking.* For example, sometimes a problem results from how your child is thinking about a situation. Perhaps Angela is frustrated with her homework and is starting to give up or argue about doing it. The reason she is starting to give up is because she is thinking negatively about her homework, especially when it is difficult. When sitting down to do her homework, she may be thinking, "I hate homework," "This will take forever," or "No one has as much homework as I do." With those thoughts taking her frontal lobes hostage, no wonder she is copping an attitude that makes Freddy Krueger look like Mr. Rogers.

You're the coach and your player needs some help in the thinking area. The way your kids think is really important,

---

*Actually three things, if you include body function noises.

because it lays the foundation for their feelings and actions. In other words, if your child's thinking goes off the tracks, so does everything else. This is part of how God made us and is why he wants us to be "made new in the attitude of your minds" (Eph. 4:23).

Angela needs to learn a skill that I call "flexible thinking." It will help her keep a God-pleasing attitude when she gets frustrated about homework. Flexible thoughts for homework could include, "I might as well just get it done," "The sooner I start, the sooner I'm done," "All my friends have homework too," or "If I get stuck, I can ask for help." Even a simple prayer, such as, "Lord, help me handle this situation the right way," will help Angela refocus and remember that she wants to obey God in every area of her life, including how she handles her homework. Filling her mind with these flexible thoughts will help Angela look at the situation from a more positive and accurate perspective, which will make it easier for her to get her homework done without breaking too many pencils.

b. *Responding.* Your child's responses include what they say and do in a situation. For example, let's say your son has developed the diabolical habit of annoying his sister by touching or, worse yet, breathing in the general direction of her food at dinner when you are not looking. However, the behavior we want to focus on here is that of the sister. What do you want *her* to say and do when her brother purposely annoys her?

Your daughter will definitely need some coaching on this one. Here's a foolproof three-step plan for responding to sibling aggravation that works much better than her usual response of name-calling, hitting, or feeding his prize-winning LEGO collection to the dog. It is divided into what to *say* and *do*:

SAY:	1. Ask him to stop in a respectful way (i.e., "Johnny, please stop touching my food.")

2. Ask him to stop again (still respectfully) but with a more serious tone (i.e., "Johnny, I asked you to *please stop* touching my food.")

DO:	3. Walk away (if applicable) and get help from parents.

Ask yourself this question: "How will she get in trouble if she sticks with this plan?" The answer is: she won't. This plan is smart and respectful, and she has a dad who is going to teach her how to do it. Lucky girl.

The areas of thinking and responding apply to any circumstance your kids will encounter. Bobby may need your coaching help to *think* positively when he makes a mistake. Rachel may need your coaching help for how to *respond* (what to say and do) to other kids in order to make friends at school. Focusing on the areas of *thinking* and *responding* will help you identify exactly where to put your coaching efforts to help your child make a good choice in any situation.

2. Teach and practice the appropriate skill. This is like Luke's quarterback coach getting on the field and showing him the proper mental steps, body posture, and footwork involved in throwing the football. A good coach doesn't just tell his players what to do; he shows them and practices with them. So choose a relaxed time and have fun coaching your child.

a. *Thinking.* For instance, if your child needs to improve at flexible thinking, I suggest you make a list of three to five flexible thoughts that you and your child will memorize together. Here are some examples:

"I should just do it."	"It's no big deal."
"It won't take that long."	"Everyone makes mistakes."
"That's okay, I can do it later."	"Sometimes you win, sometimes you lose."

Once your child has them memorized, sit down together and give your child a few practice scenarios, where she can practice thinking of two or three flexible thoughts for any situation you give her. She can use flexible thoughts from the list or she can make up her own. The scenarios should include the type of situations she has been having trouble dealing with. Here is an example of how a practice session might sound:

Dad: "Okay, Ben, here's a situation. Let's pretend that you want to stay up later at bedtime and mom says no. What are a couple of good flexible thoughts that would help you make a good choice for what to do?"

Ben: "I could think it's no big deal or that I can stay up later some other time."

Dad: "Excellent. Okay, Susie, here's one for you. Let's say you made a mistake in one of your dance routines at a dance recital. What are some flexible thoughts that would help you handle that in a positive way?"

Susie: "I could think that I tried my best and everyone makes mistakes sometimes. Plus, I can work on the dance routine and do it better next time."

Dad: "Awesome. Okay, Mom, how about if you try one. Let's say that little Tony has an ear infection, Ben is throwing up with the flu, Susie needs you to take her to dance class, and this is all happening on a weekend when I am away at a four-day business convention at the Disney World resort in Orlando. What flexible thoughts would you use?"

Mom: (dryly) "When he gets back, I'm going to Tahiti."

b. *Responding.* If you are practicing the three-step plan for responding to sibling aggravation, you would sit down with your daughter and explain the three steps. She will need you to show her how to add a more serious tone to her voice (step 2) without resorting to yelling. Then pretend to touch her food and have her practice the steps until she can do them easily. Before you know it, she'll be a pro.* Your role play might go like this:

Dad: "Okay, I'll pretend that I'm Johnny and I'm touching your food at dinner. You show me the three steps. Ready?"

Susie: "Okay."

(Dad pretends to touch Susie's food)

Susie: "Johnny, please don't touch my dinner."

Dad: "That was great. Now let's pretend that Johnny touched it again. What would you say?"

Susie: (with a more serious tone) "Johnny, I asked you to *stop* touching my dinner."

Dad: "That was awesome. It was a little stronger, but you weren't shouting. Now, if Johnny did it one more time, what would you say or do?"

Susie: "I'd say, 'Mom or Dad, Johnny is touching my dinner, and I asked him to stop, but he won't.'"

Dad: "Susie, that was perfect. Who would be getting in trouble at that point?"

Susie: "Johnny."

Dad: "Unfortunately, you are right, because he needs to respect you when you ask him to stop. Who wouldn't be getting into trouble?"

Susie: "Me?"

Dad: "That is also right. That's because you used a plan that was smart and respectful. Good job!"

You can practice plans for responding with your kids for situations they might someday find themselves in, such as

---

*Then you need to get to work on the brother.

inviting a friend to play, standing up to peer pressure, or reminding the officer that they have the right to a phone call.

Remember, you're a coach, and you want your kids to have fun learning these important life skills with their dad. The practices work the best when they are short, fun, and loaded with positive encouragement. Just like with sports, it takes more than just one practice to build a new skill, so you may need to practice your plan with your child a few times until you see the new behavior start to take place in real life. Like Radio, your kids need someone to teach them how to handle life's tough situations, someone to see the gold nugget inside of them and bring it out. Every player needs a coach. Every kid needs a great dad. Luckily for your kids, they've got both.

Key Points

1. Part of being a great dad is being a coach.
2. A referee calls penalties while a coach *teaches* his kids how to do it *right*.
3. A coach turns a problem situation into a positive skill or lesson that can be taught.
4. The first step in coaching is to identify the skill area (e.g., thinking, responding) that your child needs help with.
5. Practicing the appropriate skill helps your child improve his ability to think and respond positively to difficult situations.

Getting to Work

1. Read Proverbs 1:8–9; 16:23; 22:6; and Ephesians 6:4. Why is it so important for a dad to spend time teaching

and training his kids? What are some life skills your kids need to improve in?

2. How do you see the difference between a coach and a referee? Which one are you most like with your kids? How can you become more like a coach?

3. Name a situation where your child becomes overly frustrated, sad, or upset. Identify three flexible thoughts you can teach your child to use in that situation.

 Frustrated/sad/upset situation: _____
 Flexible thoughts:

 a) _____
 b) _____
 c) _____

4. Name a situation where your child needs help with how he or she responds. Identify a more positive, friendly, or respectful response that you can practice together.

 Problem situation: _____
 Say: _____
 Do: _____

5. Picture a fourth-grade basketball team in a gym, ready for a practice, but the coach doesn't show up. What would happen during the next forty-five minutes? How productive would it likely be? Now picture another fourth-grade basketball team in a different gym, but their coach is there, instructing the players, running drills, encouraging their progress, and having fun. How will this practice be different than that of the team with no coach? Explain how this analogy applies to your role as a coach for your kids.

Save the Picnic

Stephen King beware. Zombie fire ants are making their way to a town near you. According to an article written by Bill Hanna for the *Fort Worth Star-Telegram*, there is a tiny little fly that is turning fire ants into zombies in Texas. The phorid fly, which hails from South America, apparently enjoys nothing more than dive-bombing friendly and unsuspecting fire ants, who are busy with their day's work of stinging anything that gets in their way, and cleverly laying its eggs on the ant's thorax. All is fine until the maggot that hatches inside the ant makes its way up to the ant's head and eats his brain. Once brainless, the fire ant wanders around aimlessly for about two weeks. Until his head falls off. Scoreboard reads: Phorid fly: 1; Fire ant: 0.

You may be wondering why I am sharing this fascinating but useless information about fire ants and phorid flies with you. The reason is simple: dads who lose their temper at their kids and allow their anger to hurt their family remind me a lot of zombie fire ants. They are wandering around with their brains eaten up by anger. With their brains short-circuited, they allow their words and actions to inflict damage on the family that they love so dearly. And when their brains return to full functioning,* they realize the damage they have done and are filled with regret about the relationships they have hurt.

Why All the Anger?

A dad can get angry for a lot of reasons. It could be because he grew up in a family where he saw anger expressed inappropriately by his parents on a daily basis. It could be because he has "a short fuse" that has been a part of his personality ever since he was a kid. It could be because he is a Cubs fan.

I think the main reason dads get angry is because they care. If you have a dozen doughnuts in a carry-out box but none of them are the kind you like, you are not really bothered if you drop the box or happen to run over it with your car. However, let's say the box contains your very *favorite* doughnut, and in your rush to get home you hit a speed bump that sends the carry-out box flying into the backseat, causing the doughnuts to be ejected from the box and to land, frosting side down, on your car's floorboard, which is still fresh with mud and gravel from your kids' soccer cleats. Your favorite doughnut is now ruined. Your brain immediately floods with emotion, and you pound the steering wheel in anger as you scream out the age-old metaphysical question, "*Why?*"†

Why all the emotion? I'll tell you why. Because you *care* about that doughnut. And most dads I know care far more about their kids than they do about their doughnuts. (*Most* dads.) When the child you care about makes a bad choice, it

---

*The fire ants are not this lucky.

†Of course, you will still eat the doughnut.

148

impacts your emotions. The irony is that when your anger is aroused, its destructive force can disconnect your brain and cause you to damage the very thing you care the most about. As Proverbs 14:17 reminds us, "A quick-tempered man does foolish things."

There Goes the Picnic

In *The Five Love Language of Teenagers*, Gary Chapman points out that negative anger expression by a parent can carry even more weight than the parent's positive efforts. Just the encouraging news we needed to hear. Talking about teens, Chapman writes, "The teenager who is verbally or physically abused by an angry parent will no longer remember the acts of service, words of affirmation, quality time, gifts, and physical touch that were received in childhood. All they will remember are the cutting words of rebuke and condemnation and the screaming voice of their parent. They feel no love, only painful rejection."[1]

The negative impact of a dad's inappropriately expressed anger is devastating. It doesn't just damage the bridge we talked about in chapter 9; it loads it with TNT and blows it up. It treats your kids with *dis*respect and shows them the double standard that yelling and the use of hurtful words are okay if you are the dad, but not if you are the kid. It shuts down the lines of communication and makes your kids think twice before they decide if they are going to tell you about a mistake they made or an issue they need help with.

Nobody wants fire ants at their picnic. No doubt about it, a great dad does not give himself permission to be a zombie fire ant, even if he comes from a long line of zombie fire ants. Regardless of the reasons that he is angry, a great dad will remember that love "is not easily angered" (1 Cor. 13:5). He will do what it takes to handle his frustration in a way that values and protects his connection with his kids. He will be a coach who will turn problem situations into positive lessons, not angry tirades.

In other words, he won't ruin the picnic.

Controlling Your Anger

All of us get mad at our kids from time to time.* The strategies below will be simple enough for every dad to use and yet powerful enough to help you if your anger has become a larger problem. The Bible tells us that it is better to be a patient man than a warrior, better to be a man who controls his temper than one who takes a city (see Prov. 16:32). Here are three strategies for being a great dad instead of a zombie fire ant.

1. *Use flexible thoughts.* In the last chapter I introduced you to flexible thoughts as a wonderful skill to teach your kids. I have great news: they work just as well for dads.

John was a thirty-five-year-old dad whose ten-year-old son, Peter, was getting the best of him. As we sat together in my office, we talked about a recent situation where John had blown his fuse when Peter argued about getting ready for bed. We examined what John was *thinking* during Peter's misbehavior and here's what it was: *Why can't that kid listen for once? Does he have to ruin every bedtime? After being at work all day, I have to end my night like this?* If we took these thoughts and inserted them into the pope's head, he'd be angry at Peter too. John had let his thinking become dominated by *mad* thoughts instead of *flexible* thoughts.

As John and I identified flexible thoughts that he could have used in that situation, a look of relief came over his face. "These would have been so helpful," he told me, "because they're *true.*" Flexible thoughts simply remind you of what is true. Of the big picture. Of what is really important. Here are a few flexible thoughts that I use when frustration knocks:

*Such as getting-dressed time, after-school time, clean-up-your-room time, put-your-toys-away time, turn-off-the-TV time, get-ready-for-bed time, and so on.

150

FLEXIBLE DAD THOUGHTS

"My job is to be a coach and help _____ (child's name) learn the right lesson."	"The Family Respect Rule applies to me *right now*."
"I want to show my kids how to handle frustration the way God wants us to."	"I do not want to damage my most valuable relationships with my anger."
"I want to be respectful even if I'm frustrated."	"Lord, help me handle this in a way that honors you."
"I want to turn this into the best learning situation for _____ (child's name) that I can."	"The calmer I am, the better I'll handle it."

Focusing on these thoughts will not take your frustration away entirely; they're not supposed to. But they will reduce your frustration to a level that doesn't turn you into a zombie fire ant, so that you can be an effective coach for your kids.

Here's what I suggest. Choose three "flexible dad thoughts" from this list, or if you'd prefer, make up some of your own. Then memorize them. It is also a great idea to memorize a few key thoughts from Scripture, such as "The fruit of the Spirit is . . . gentleness and self-control" (Gal. 5:22–23); "Love is patient, love is kind. . . . It is not easily angered" (1 Cor. 13:4–5); or "for man's anger does not bring about the righteous life that God desires" (James 1:20).

When you have chosen the thoughts you want to memorize, drill them into your brain until you say them in your sleep. In your prayer times, ask God to help you stay focused on becoming the great dad he wants you to be, even when you are frustrated. As you train your brain to be flexible and you fill your mind with God's Word, you will find that your inner zombie fire ant will begin to disappear.

2. *Control your anger "on the spot."* Here are five "on the spot" tips for what to do when you feel the anger rising:

a. *Pause.* A short pause has saved me more than once. Pausing at the first sign of anger shows control and intentionality rather than uncensored reaction. It demonstrates that you actually do have more self-control than an aggressive hamster. *What should I do when I pause?* you ask. I take two or three deep breaths and get my mind focused on the flexible thoughts I have memorized. Darth Vader is attacking and you, Luke Skywalker, must use your flexible thought lightsaber to fight him off and win the battle.*

b. *Focus on the lesson.* I use this one a lot. When kids misbehave, there is a lesson to be learned, and a great dad will get right to it. Just ask yourself, "What is the lesson my kids need to learn in this situation?" Remember, you are a coach, and your job is to teach. Focus on the lesson that God wants you to teach your kids and how to teach it the right way and you'll be too busy being a great dad to be a zombie fire ant.

c. *Take a short break.* Sometimes the anger rushes in pretty fast and it is hard to think clearly. No problem. Just take a short break to cool down. All you need to say is, "I'm pretty frustrated and I need to cool down for a minute. I'll be right back." Then get to a quiet place (i.e., step outside, go to your room) where you can take a few deep breaths and ask God to help you get your thoughts refocused on what is important. When you rejoin the conversation, you'll be a much more effective coach.

d. *Decide later.* I don't know about you, but for me, it is not always easy to think of the perfect negative consequence in the heat of a frustrating moment. There have been several times when I have given a quick negative consequence only to think of a much better negative consequence a few minutes later.

For example, I remember a few years ago when Jake had not cleaned his room after being asked to several times. "Okay, I guess we'll be taking a break from computer and video games," I quickly said as I left his room and walked downstairs. Not entirely satisfied with my response, I sat down at the kitchen table and took a moment to think. *What's the best way to handle this?* I wondered to myself. *What consequence*

---

*I work with kids eight hours a day—what do you expect?

will help him learn the right lesson? I got up and poured my-self some orange juice, pondering my negative consequence options (you'll learn about them in chapter 16).

Then it hit me.

"Jake," I called.

"Yeah, Dad," he answered as he walked to the hallway and looked down at me over the landing.

"I've thought about it and decided what your consequence will be."

"I thought you said it was computer and video games."

"Well, I've decided to change it a little."

"Okay, what is it?"

"Well, you have to learn to keep your room clean and to do it when Mom or I ask you. So step one will be to clean your room immediately. If you're not sure how to do it or where to put something, just ask me and I'll be glad to help you out. However, since you've had such a hard time getting this done, this tells me you need a little room-cleaning practice. So after you have cleaned up your room properly, you will also clean up your brother's room. And yes, there will be no computer or video games until this is all done."

We haven't had a lot of room-cleaning problems since.

So if you are sure that a negative consequence is in order but are not sure what that consequence should be, just tell your child that there *will* be a consequence and that you are going to think about it first before you decide. Sometimes it is appropriate to discuss the situation with your wife before you make a decision so that you can choose a consequence together. Either way, knowing that you are going to think about it should leave them quaking in their boots.

e. *Do no harm.* The Latin phrase *primum non nocere* means "First, do no harm." It is commonly taught to all medical students, along with the Latin phrase *Tamen is est okay inhaero populus per porro cuspis postulo*, which means "But it is okay to stick people with long pointed needles." If your anger is brimming over and you are on the verge of saying or doing something hurtful, then focus on this one thing: *do no harm*. Excuse yourself from the situation immediately, and if possible, take a walk and cool down.

3. *Talk about it.* If you have hurt a family relationship connection with your anger, I strongly encourage you to *genuinely* apologize to the offended parties. In case you are wondering, I have apologized to my boys more than once for the way I handled a situation. Hurting your family relationships with your anger is not okay, and apologizing is the first and necessary step toward repair and healing.

If you are a dad who struggles with anger, then I encourage you not to struggle alone. If you are married, talk honestly with your wife about your desire to change your angry responses. There may be ways that she can help you recognize your anger cues and use the ideas presented in this chapter. If you have a close guy friend or belong to an accountability group, tell them about your anger struggles so that they can pray with you and hold you accountable for taking the right steps. If needed, talk to your pastor or to a qualified therapist who can teach you how to put these steps to work and help you uncover the obstacles that have been getting in your way. You may need to talk to your family physician to consider whether medication can play a role on your road to getting control of your anger.

God created you to be a great dad, not a zombie fire ant. A great dad will do whatever it takes to make sure that his anger does not hurt those he loves the most. By using flexible thoughts, controlling your anger "on the spot," and talking with the right people, you can make your kids proud by taking the steps you need to take to get your emotions back on the right track. It's going to be a great picnic after all.

Key Points

1. Hurtful anger expression can overshadow your past positive interactions.

2. A dad's anger can put TNT on the relationship bridge and blow it up.
3. Learning to use flexible thoughts and memorize Scripture is an important way to manage everyday frustration.
4. Pausing and taking a break are effective ways to stop your anger from gaining momentum.
5. Talking about your anger with your wife, a friend, your pastor, or a counselor can be the first step to victory.

Getting to Work

1. How did you see anger expressed in your home as a child? What was your dad's style of handling anger when you were a kid? How has it impacted your style of handling anger now?
2. Read Proverbs 14:17; 15:1; 29:11; 1 Corinthians 13:4–7; and James 1:19–20. What do these verses teach us about the way a father should handle his frustration with his kids? What are some anger behaviors that harm your relationship bridge? What impact will these negative behaviors have on your kids?
3. Choose a combination of three flexible dad thoughts and/or Scripture verses that you want to memorize. Why did you choose those particular ones?
4. Which of the five "on the spot" anger control techniques will help you the most when you need to stay in control of your rising temper?
5. Have you ever apologized to your kids when your anger response was inappropriate? Who can you talk to about anger-related issues when you need to? Are there any steps toward controlling your anger that you need to take today?

Find the Horse

There's an old story about a dad who had two boys: one was an extreme pessimist, the other an extreme optimist. Worried about the extreme differences in their personalities, the dad did what any self-respecting dad would do. He took them to a psychologist.

The psychologist took the pessimistic boy into a room filled with brand-new toys, still in their original packaging, expecting him to be thrilled. "Oh no," wailed the boy as he burst into tears. "What's wrong?" asked the psychologist, baffled by the boy's response. "It will take so long to open all these toys and read the directions," the boy cried, "and then they'll probably break."

The psychologist then took the optimistic boy into a room piled five feet high with horse manure, expecting him to recoil at the repulsive sight and smell. Instead, the boy let out a yelp of glee as he jumped into the pile of manure and started digging away. "What on earth are you doing?" the psychologist asked. The little boy, covered with manure, looked up at him and with a big grin said, "With all this manure, there's got to be a horse in here somewhere."

As dads, one thing we know for sure is that our kids will face many difficult challenges: being on a losing sports team, being excluded by a group of friends, or (brace yourself) not having the very latest cell phone. The last thing we want is for our kids to develop the habit of giving up when faced with a problem. When I see a child who feels like giving up on a problem, I see a child who thinks the problem is bigger than he or she is. That is certainly how it feels. I am very familiar with this feeling, as I experience it every time I try to add fabric softener to the laundry.

As great dads, our job is to help our kids develop a positive way of thinking about and responding to everyday problems. Jesus told us that we will all face problems and obstacles: "He causes his sun to rise on the evil and the good, and sends rain on the righteous and the unrighteous" (Matt. 5:45). But as the apostle Paul (who was stoned, imprisoned, flogged, shipwrecked, and often a victim of slow service at the local deli) wrote, "in all these things we are more than conquerors through him who loved us" (Rom. 8:37).

A great dad will teach his kids that there is no pile of manure that God can't help them hop over, find a way around, or if need be, wade through. And more than that, some piles may actually have a horse hidden inside for those who know how to find it. So I invite you to put your galoshes on and your nose plugs in as I show you two great strategies for helping your kids find the horse.

Strategy #1: Look at It Another Way

A four-year-old went with his pregnant mother to her doctor's appointment. Sitting in the waiting room, the mother suddenly appeared startled and clutched her stomach. "Mommy, what is it?" the boy asked. "The baby brother you're going to have is kicking," the mom explained with a smile. "He's probably restless," the boy said. "Why don't you swallow a toy?"[1]

Now that's the kind of thinking that will get you elected president of the United States. We want our kids to learn how to look at problem situations in a creative way. In his book *A Whack on the Side of the Head*, Roger von Oech offers a couple great ideas that we can use to stimulate our kids' creative, optimistic thinking that will help them look at their challenges another way.[2]

1. *Change the question.* When you can't find a way around a problem you are facing, von Oech recommends changing the questions you are asking. Allow me to illustrate. Let's say that Jack plays baseball and has become discouraged because he has struck out a few times. Unfortunately for Jack, the only question bouncing around in his head is, "Why is this happening to me?" This question sends his imagination into a negative tailspin as he pictures himself as the first kid listed in the *Guinness Book of World Records* for striking out every time he goes to bat for the rest of his life. As long as Jack is stuck on this question, there is as much hope for him as there is for an oven-fresh chocolate éclair at an Overeaters Anonymous meeting.

Little does Jack realize that his biggest problem is not that he has struck out a few times but that he is stuck on the wrong question. Now, being dads who are programmed by our DNA to fix things and fix them fast, our temptation will be to tell Jack not only the questions he should be asking but the answers as well. You must fight your inner repairman urge and instead start by giving Jack a chance to tell you how he feels about his situation, as we discussed in chapter 11. Once his truck is fully unloaded, *then* you can gently tell him you have a few questions that might be helpful. You might say something like this: "Jack, as you were talking, a couple questions came to mind that might help. Can I run them past you?"

In Jack's case, helpful questions might include the following:

- Besides hitting, have you made any good plays for your team this year?
- Do any other kids on your team (in your league, at your age) ever strike out?
- Do you realize that you could still have a career with the Chicago Cubs?
- Do kids older than you ever strike out?
- Do professional baseball players ever strike out?
- What do you think the pros do when they are in a batting slump?
- Have you talked to the coach about your batting?
- If you want to improve your batting, what is a good step you can take?

Changing the questions your kids are asking when they are faced with a problem takes their focus out of a destructive place and puts it in a productive place. The question "Why am I such a *loser?*" does not lead to any productive answers. However, helping your kids ask the *right* questions frees them up to look at their situation from a different perspective, refocuses them on the positive facts they have been overlooking, and stimulates positive ideas for action that will help them get moving in the right direction.

2. *Use your imagination.* Another strategy von Oech suggests is to use your imagination to picture how *someone else* would handle the obstacle you are facing. I have found this idea to be useful, or at least amusing, on many occasions, such as imagining how my wife would kill the big spider in the corner.* Robby was a twelve-year-old boy who came to see me because he had been teased by a couple kids at school. I was afraid that Robby's emotional response would keep

*Dowse the corner with gasoline and set it on fire.

the teasers coming back for more. So I had Robby use his imagination to picture how one of his friends might handle the exact same situation.

> Me: "Robby, tell me the name of one of your friends who doesn't get teased much."
>
> Robby: "I've never seen Dillon get teased."
>
> Me: "Okay, we'll use Dillon as our example. Now, I want you to pretend that Dillon is getting teased by the same guys that tease you. Use your imagination and picture it happening. Then picture how Dillon would respond. Picture what Dillon would say and do."
>
> Robby: "He'd probably just say, 'Whatever, dude,' and walk away."
>
> Me: "That's all?"
>
> Robby: "Yeah."
>
> Me: "How do you think that would work?"
>
> Robby: "Probably pretty good."

Bingo. Robby had his plan. Looking at the situation another way by imagining how someone else would handle it opened up Robby's creativity and allowed him to come up with an effective response to his problem.

By the way, it worked.

Strategy #2: Look for the Second Right Answer

Another creative strategy for overcoming an obstacle is problem solving. Von Oech describes a simple version of problem solving that he calls looking for the second right answer. That's right, the *second* right answer. This is going to bother you math teachers out there, I know. But when faced with a problem, most kids pick the first idea that pops into their heads, and then their brains immediately go back into sleep mode. For instance:

Problem: Sister bugs you.

Solution: Hit sister.

That's it. Instead, we want our kids to keep the creative thinking process going and develop the habit of looking for the second right answer. That would look like this:

Problem: Sister bugs you.

Solution #1: Hit sister.

Solution #2: Throw hard object at sister.

Clearly much better.

Problem solving is a skill that every boy and girl needs to learn. Why? Because they are faced with life-threatening problems all the time, such as not being able to stay up late on a school night. When faced with such a situation, it is easy for kids to get their minds so stuck on their problem that they don't even try to look for a solution. They blame others, give up, assume the government is secretly behind their problems,* and accomplish nothing. A great dad will teach his kids how to get their minds off of the problem and on to the solution.

In *How to Succeed in the Game of Life*, Christian Klemash asked Tony Dungy, Super Bowl–winning coach of the Indianapolis Colts, "What's the best advice you were ever given?" Dungy answered, "I've gotten a lot of good advice over the years, but I think probably the best advice I got was from my dad, when he always told me not to complain about problems and look for solutions."[3] I personally suspect the best advice Dungy ever got was, "Never, ever, under *any* circumstance fire Peyton Manning," but that is just a hunch for which I have no proof. Either way, here is a two-step problem-solving plan that will help your kids find the horse in any pile of doo-doo that life sends their way.

---

*That part is true.

Step one: Show them you understand. Trying to problem-solve before your child is ready is like trying to give rectal medicine to a 150-pound Rottweiler who doesn't really see the need for it. Once again, the first step is to show them that you understand how they feel about the situation by taking the time to let them unload their truck. After you have listened to their feelings about their problem, an empathic statement is a great way to show your kids that you have listened and understand how they feel:

- "So Jack, if I've listened right, you're feeling really discouraged about striking out the last few times, and you're afraid you might keep on striking out forever."
- "Melanie, you're telling me that you are really upset about your score on your biology test, especially because you wanted to do well and studied so hard for it."
- "Lucy, it sounds like you're feeling shocked and hurt by the way Allison treated you yesterday at the party, and you're not sure what to think of her right now."

Step two: Find the horse. Once your kids know that you have taken the time to really understand the situation from their perspective, they will be much more open to exploring possible ways to handle it. This simply involves making a list of good ideas to choose from. You can even write them down if you want. The ideas can include ways to *think* about the problem from a different perspective or ideas for *responding* to the problem (things to say or do). Here are a couple examples of common problems and the types of solutions that you and your kids might come up with:

Problem #1: A child teasing her at school
  Ideas:

  1. Think, "This happens to everyone sometimes" and "If I handle it the right way, it will eventually stop."

2. Say, "Whatever" or "That's your opinion," and walk away.
3. Read a book with my parents on how to handle teasing and talk about it together.
4. Practice how to respond to teasing with Mom or Dad.
5. Walk with my friends whenever possible.
6. Talk to Mom and Dad about it and to the school counselor if needed.
7. Ask God to give me strength and wisdom, and pray for the person teasing me.

Problem #2: Struggling in a skill-based activity (e.g., sport, musical instrument, etc.)
   Ideas:

1. Think, "I can't expect things to always be easy" and "Nobody wins all the time."
2. Remember that people who excel at an activity have spent *many* hours practicing, often for years.
3. Quit the activity and spend more time playing video games.*
4. Talk to my coach/teacher about how I can improve.
5. Ask parents for specific feedback from practices, games, or performances.
6. Tape and review my practices, performances, recitals, or competitions.
7. Talk with parents about whether I should try something different (e.g., a different sport, position, or instrument).
8. Significantly increase my practice time for one month and see if it helps.
9. Talk to someone who is really good at the activity and find out how they got there and how long it took them.

*Just joking.

10. Ask God to show me what lessons he wants me to learn from this challenge.

Of course, you won't use every good idea you think of, but your creative hunt will help your kids realize that there are more good ideas than they originally thought existed. You will also have a list to go back to if the problem doesn't get solved on your first try.

Finally, every problem situation is one that you can pray about with your kids. You can pray together for wisdom, for courage, for calmness, for perseverance, for the other people involved, and for God's hand to guide the situation. If your child is comfortable, you can pray for the situation during your family times as well and reflect on how God has helped all of you conquer problems in the past.

As you can see, there are many good ideas for how your kids can handle any problem that blocks their path. Changing the question, using their imagination, looking for the second right answer, and praying together will help them respond to problems in a way that builds their trust in God and leads them toward wise responses. Even a great kid runs into a giant pile of manure from time to time, and a great dad will be standing by with his shovel, because you just never know where you might find a horse.

Key Points

1. Every child runs into problems of many different sizes.
2. Changing the question your child is asking is a great way of helping him or her look at the problem from a different perspective.
3. Imagining how someone else might handle a challenge can help your child think of creative solutions.
4. Looking for the second right answer means making a list of ways to think about or respond to a challenge.

5. Praying together reminds your kids that God cares about and is involved in every detail of their lives.

Getting to Work

1. Read Matthew 5:43–48; John 9:1–3; Romans 8:35–39; and Hebrews 12:7–11. Why does God allow challenges and hardships to come into our lives? How does he use these "negative" situations for good?
2. Can you think of a time when one of your kids was stuck on the wrong question? What are a few of the right questions that would have helped him or her in that situation?
3. What are some situations where you can help your kids use their imagination to solve a problem at home, at school, or with friends? How might this technique help *you* in your effort to become a great dad?
4. Why is it important to show your kids you understand *before* you try to find the horse? Choose a problem that one of your kids is having or that you are running into as a family. Pick a time this week when you will have a problem-solving discussion with that child or together as a family.
5. If you show your kids how to change the question, use their imagination, look for the second right answer, and spend time praying together about the challenges they face, how will that help them handle those challenges in a way that gives glory to God?

Discipline with the End in Mind

(Not That End)

You know the story. Rocky Balboa was a small-time Philadelphia boxer and, how shall we say, loan collector. However, he had a heart made of titanium and could take a beating like no other human being who has ever lived. Having been given a shot at the World Heavyweight Championship in a media stunt by Apollo Creed, Rocky stunned the boxing world by taking more hits than the George Foreman Grill website and actually going the distance with the champ.

In order for there to be a sequel, Apollo had to offer Rocky a rematch, so in *Rocky II* that's exactly what he did. However, Rocky's trainer, Mickey, knew that with his current fighting style, Rocky had no chance of beating Apollo in a rematch. Mickey's solution was for Rocky, who was a southpaw, to learn to fight right-handed. This would help Rocky surprise

Apollo with a perfectly timed left-handed to right-handed switch and give him a chance to win.

Learning to fight right-handed was discouraging for Rocky, as he tied his left hand to his body and clumsily tried to punch with his right hand. However, once Rocky got the go-ahead from Adrian,* he turned on his unflappable willpower, turned up his Bill Conti workout music from the *Rocky* soundtrack (Da da daaaa, da da daaaa . . .), and saw the genius of Mickey's plan start to materialize. Rocky was transformed into a powerful ambidextrous fighter who defeated his overconfident opponent and became the new heavyweight champion of the world.

The "End" of Discipline

Welcome to the topic of discipline. Rocky had developed some terribly bad boxing habits, not the least of which was the often underappreciated strategy of blocking punches with his face. I am not a boxing aficionado, but I'm pretty sure that was not a strategy Muhammad Ali used. Rocky's bad habits would have caused him not just to lose his rematch with Apollo but probably to get his head knocked into the outer orbit of Jupiter. To avoid this unpleasant outcome, Mickey's plan (e.g., learning to fight right-handed) was not necessarily fun, but neither was it intended to be punitive. It was designed with a specific end in mind: to beat Apollo. Mickey's "discipline" made Rocky's victory possible.

As you can see, in this chapter I want to stretch the way you think about discipline. In chapter 13 we talked about how a coach teaches his players how to do things *right*. In this chapter we're going to talk about what the coach should do when his players do things *wrong*. Of course, a good coach needs to do both of these, and I will show you how to

---

*Never participate in a life-threatening fight without your wife's approval.

blend it all together to help your kids experience the result of doing things wrong and learn the skills to do it right. Just as Mickey did with Rocky, we are going to think of discipline as a teaching technique, because that's really what it is. Effective discipline is designed to teach a lesson. As your kids' coach, you have many lessons you want them to learn:

- The value of obeying their parents
- The value of being honest
- The value of working hard
- The value of communicating their ideas in a respectful way
- The value of asking mom if she's been losing weight lately

The author of Hebrews tells us, "No discipline seems pleasant at the time, but painful. Later on, however, it produces a harvest of righteousness and peace for those who have been trained by it" (Heb. 12:11). Did you notice the last three words? The purpose of discipline is *training*. The training that discipline brings is necessary if your kids are going to learn to make the kind of choices that will keep them on God's path and out of the principal's office. As with coaching, the "end" of discipline can be stated very simply: to help your kids learn the right lessons, the right way.

Part of Every Coach's Job

The kids on a basketball team know they need a coach. You don't often hear them say, "Hey, who's this guy with the funny shorts telling us what to do? Get him outta here." The kids are counting on the coach's knowledge and experience to lead them. They know that they have no chance of winning without him. The coach is their leader. He will teach. He will encourage. He will fall asleep on the bus.

He will also discipline.

For example, if they run out of steam by halftime, the players know they will run extra "suicides" or "killers"* in the next practice to improve their conditioning. This is the "consequence" of their poor performance from the game before, but it is also designed to improve their endurance for the next game. If they shoot poorly in a game, they will do extra shooting drills in the next practice. If a player shows poor sportsmanship or treats others disrespectfully, that player will take a seat on the bench until he or she decides to start treating others respectfully. These are all examples of the coach teaching important lessons through thoughtful discipline. This is part of every coach's job. This is part of every great dad's job too.

When I talk with fathers about discipline, our discussion inevitably gets broken down into the two areas that comprise a dad's role in every discipline situation: content and style. *Content* refers to your choice of consequences. *Style* refers to the way you administer those consequences. A great dad will learn to administer effective consequences with a relationship-building style. To say it again, he'll teach the right lessons, the right way.

Choosing the Right Content

You have many choices when it comes to consequences. The way to choose the wrong consequence is to act like a zombie fire ant and let your anger dictate your actions and decisions. Bad idea. The way to choose the right consequence is to think like a wise coach who wants his player to learn an important lesson.

The word *consequence* simply means result. As the coach, you have the job of deciding what result will help your child learn the right lesson from his or her bad choice. You have a lot of consequence options that can be used by themselves

*Undoubtedly named by a dad.

or in combination to teach your kids the right lesson. The consequences should influence how your kids think about their behavior, improve their skill in handling a situation respectfully, and increase their motivation to make a more respectful choice next time. While it is impossible for me to be exhaustive, allow me to give you a master idea list that you can use to think of effective consequences for any situation:

Master Idea List That You Can Use to Think of Effective Consequences for Any Situation

- Give a warning or reminder.
- Use a negative consequence that is logically related to the situation (e.g., removing a privilege, enforcing an early bedtime, etc.).
- Have your child do 200 push-ups.
- Use the situation as a springboard for a family time discussion.
- Do some problem solving with your child to figure out how to prevent this problem in the future, as discussed in chapter 15.
- Have your child take a time-out.
- Discuss an applicable Bible verse together to see what lesson God can teach you and your child through this mistake.
- Make a plan for how your child can respond (what they can *say* and *do*) in that situation in the future and practice that plan, as discussed in chapter 13.
- Teach your child a plan for how to cool down "on the spot" when feeling upset, using ideas from chapter 14 (e.g., pause, use flexible thoughts, ask for a break).
- Pray with your child about the situation.
- Have your child do 500 push-ups.*

---

*Just joking about the push-ups. However, if *you* want to have ripped pecs, do 50 push-ups each time your wife reminds you to put the toilet seat down.

- Have your child write a paragraph about the importance of _____ (e.g., honesty, treating others respectfully, etc.).
- If anger was an issue, practice using flexible thoughts with your child, as discussed in chapter 13.
- Have your child make appropriate apologies.
- Identify the flexible thought that would have helped your child make a better choice and have him write it twenty-five times. Neatly.
- Make a list of the benefits of handling a certain situation respectfully and the costs of handling it disrespectfully.

You will notice that this is not a list of punishments. Instead, it is a list of discipline responses, designed to teach your kids two important things:

1. Disrespectful behavior does not pay off.
2. Dad and Mom love you enough to teach you how to handle things better next time.

As I mentioned, in some situations you will use only one of these ideas. In other situations you will choose to combine several ideas together. Just as Mickey's creative plan helped Rocky win the title, the consequences you choose will help your kids learn the valuable lesson that disrespectful behavior doesn't pay off and will help them improve at the thinking and responding they need to make a better choice next time. *Important reminder*: As your child's coach, it is important to remember that you may not be the *only* coach on the field. If you are married, it is always a good idea to talk together with your wife about the consequences for a situation. This will help you create an atmosphere of marital teamwork, come up with the most effective ideas, and show your kids how a great dad and a great mom work together.

It's All in the Style

Your style refers to the *way* you give negative consequences to your kids. Bad news time: most dads I know have blown it in the style area. Even really great dads. Even though I am fairly mild-tempered by nature, I have blown it in the style area a few times myself. Remember the relationship bridge we talked about in chapter 9 (the one you *don't* want to damage)? One of the most common assaults on that bridge comes from a parent's negative style when disciplining his or her kids.

Proverbs 29:11 tells us that "A fool gives full vent to his anger, but a wise man keeps himself under control." A negative discipline style eclipses the positive power of your coaching lesson and puts all the attention on your anger and *lack* of self-control. Your child is no longer thinking about the lesson she needs to learn; she is instead wondering if she should call the SWAT team for backup. She is learning the lesson that yelling, put-downs, interrupting, and refusing to listen to what anyone else has to say are okay if you are a grownup. Wrong lesson.

On the other hand, a warm and respectful discipline style from a dad is amazing. It shows your kids what God-centered testosterone looks like. It communicates that there are rules and boundaries in your family that will be enforced and lessons that are important enough to be taught. And it shows your kids that you refuse to damage your relationship with them while you do the enforcing and teaching. Your warm and controlled style shows them that you are a loving coach who wants to teach them an important lesson, not a referee who just doles out punishment. It reminds your kids that you have not forgotten the Family Respect Rule and that they are still worth far more than a thousand-dollar bill to you. Take a look at these examples:

GOOD: (calmly) "Johnny, it is never okay to hit your brother. Because of that, I want you to go sit in time-out. When you are done, we can talk about what happened."

GOOD: (calmly) "Katie, because you have argued so much about bedtime, there will be a consequence. Mom and I will talk about it, and I'll let you know what we decide."

GOOD: (calmly) "Michael, because of all that arguing about turning off the video game earlier today, there will be no video or computer games for you tomorrow. This also shows me that you need some practice with your flexible thoughts. So here's what we'll do. I want you to neatly write 'It's no big deal, I can play it later' twenty-five times on this sheet of paper, because this is a flexible thought that you really could have used. Pal, I'm hoping that this little exercise will help you remember to use your flexible thoughts the next time Mom asks you to turn the video game off."

BAD: (with New York mobster accent) "All right, little missy, you're grounded from your cell phone, and now that I think about it, you're grounded from the computer too. In fact, I think your little goldfish better start watching his back—I'd hate for him to have some kind of accident, if you know what I mean."

Keeping your discipline style respectful and self-controlled will help you keep your focus on the "end" of discipline, which is to teach the right lessons, *the right way*. It will protect the relationship bridge you have worked so hard to build with the kids you love so much. When you take the time to discipline thoughtfully by choosing the right consequences and responding with a loving and respectful style, you will become the coach of the year. Maybe of the century. And your kids and family will be the winners. If you were Rocky's coach, Apollo had better beware.

Key Points

1. The "end" or goal of discipline is to help your kids learn the right lessons, the right way.
2. Discipline includes two components: content and style.
3. The consequences you choose should be designed to teach your kids how to handle a situation respectfully and increase their motivation to do so.
4. A negative discipline style will damage your relationship connection with your child.
5. A loving and respectful discipline style reminds your kids how important they are to you even when you are frustrated with their behavior.

Getting to Work

1. Read Proverbs 19:18; Hebrews 12:11; and Revelation 3:19. What do these verses tell us about the "end" or purpose of discipline?
2. Page 171 lists two important lessons that discipline can teach. How is this different from punishment?
3. Why is it so important to choose the right consequences or content? What can happen if you choose the wrong ones?
4. What kind of discipline style did your parents use with you? How would you describe your discipline style today? What is one way you can improve your style?
5. Let's practice. Choose a negative behavior from one of your kids and, using the list of consequences on pages 170–71, create a combination of negative consequences that will help your child learn the right lesson, the right way.

PART 5

How You Lead Your Children

Follow My Lead

Today my friend David is taking his fifteen-year-old son Cole on a twenty-hour drive (one way) to the mountains of Colorado, where they will spend ten days forging through the forest with one objective in mind: to kill an elk with a bow and arrow. Most of my friends who enjoy hunting would gladly give a minor appendage to go on a trip like this. I, on the other hand, consider myself to have successfully lived through a life-endangering hunting expedition when I pick up a stick of beef jerky at 7-Eleven.

However, David's main mission on this trip is to set his sights not on an elk but on his son. In fact, he quipped to me something that his father had told him: "Never let school get in the way of your child's education." David plans to use this time to bond with Cole, have some meaningful father-son talks, and make memories that will last almost as long as my beef jerky.

But this is not to say that there are not real dangers on this trip, and David is well aware of them. In fact, I know that he will take every possible safety precaution, such as having Cole carry bear mace (I'm not joking) in case a bear tries to mug them. As they make their way through the mountains, David will be leading the way. He'll determine the safest path to take. He'll go first and Cole will follow, watching his dad's every step. David won't *tell* Cole to clean and quarter a five-hundred-pound elk while he rustles up a tasty leaf and bug salad; they'll do the nasty job *together*. Cole will learn a lot about hunting and camping on this trip by watching his dad. He'll learn a lot about life every other day of his life by doing the same thing.

Beverly Hills Bobo

Social psychologist Albert Bandura is famous for his "Bobo doll" experiments (named after Bobo the clown) where children watched a film of an adult hitting and kicking an inflatable clown and then were given an inflatable clown to play with. Guess what they did? They beat the living daylights out of the inflatable clown. So what's the big deal about that? The big deal for the researchers at Stanford in the early 1960s was that the kids' behavior was altered *without* the use of rewards. In other words, their behavior was changed just by *watching*.

Bandura referred to this as modeling, and it is a concept that a great dad will keep in the forefront of his mind. I remember the first time I saw *Beverly Hills Cop*. I was twenty-two years old and, like the rest of my friends, thought that Eddie Murphy's fast-talking and foul-mouthed performance was actually pretty cool and funny. But then an interesting thing started to happen: I noticed that my internal mental dialogue started to sound a lot like Murphy's obscenity-laden language. A joke would come to my mind, but now it would have a profanity embedded in it. When I got frustrated, profanity flowed effortlessly through my frontal lobes. As a guy who cussed as often as the Detroit Lions have won a Super Bowl,* this invasion of swear words in my mind seemed as out of place as Sylvester Stallone at a tongue-twister convention. Where did this sudden infusion of foul language come from? I think Bandura's Bobo doll might know the answer.

Keep in mind that I did not watch *Beverly Hills Cop* twenty-four hours a day. I saw it once, maybe twice. That's a grand total of about three or four hours of my time. Yet my internal "thinking language" had been powerfully impacted. You've probably heard of The Learning Channel (otherwise known as TLC), host of such quality shows as *American Chopper* and my wife's personal favorite, *Cake Boss*. Well, you *are* the learning channel for your kids, with no commercial breaks. The impact that a few hours of Eddie Murphy had on the quality of my thought life makes me shudder when I think about the thousands of hours my boys have been watching me. And they're not done watching yet. The good thing is that I get to choose what they are going to see next.

A Living Picture

Modeling is not Bandura's creation; he simply discovered that God designed our brains to learn by watching. This is why Jesus actually lived *with* his disciples for three years instead of teaching them six hours a day and then getting his own suite at the Galilee Hilton each night. They were learning from Jesus *each second* they were with him. Not just during the teaching moments recorded in Scripture, but during all the unrecorded times as well: their meals, their travel times, and their leisure times. They watched and learned from Jesus when they fed the five thousand, listened to the Sermon on the Mount, and ate carry-out pizza around the campfire on a Friday night.

Paul told the Corinthian believers to "Follow my example, as I follow the example of Christ" (1 Cor. 11:1). He knew

*Never.

179

that they needed a living picture to look at in order to best learn how to follow Christ in their daily lives, and he volunteered for the job. In the lives of your children, God has given you the job of being that living picture. That is why Deuteronomy 6 tells us to seize the times with our children, as we discussed in chapter 4. Your kids are always watching and being influenced by you, whether they know it or not—and whether you know it or not.

In a sense we have been talking about modeling through much of this book already, as we have focused on the influence you will have on your kids by communicating warmly, being a good listener, prioritizing relationships, being respectful, controlling your anger, and so on. Your kids will learn the value of making wise choices in these important areas by watching your example. In this chapter, however, I want to touch on two other critical areas where your children will follow your lead: your spiritual life and your marriage.

Your Spiritual Life

I must confess something right now: I am a huge fan of the television show *24*. In case you've missed it, *24* is the story of Jack Bauer, a patriotic counterterrorism agent who gets caught in unbelievably impossible situations as he races against the clock, bureaucratic red tape, and even political treason to stop a string of massive terrorist attacks against the United States. And he has to do it within twenty-four hours.

You can take all of the Chuck Norris jokes you've heard (such as "Superman wears Chuck Norris pajamas" or "Chuck Norris doesn't sleep, he waits") and just replace Chuck Norris's name with Jack Bauer. As my boys would say, Jack Bauer is *the man*. This show should win *every* Emmy award every year, including all previous Emmy awards since 1809. My boys and I have spent many hours together marveling at Jack's creative genius at finding and trapping the bad guys. If it weren't for Jack, the United States would be shredded wheat by now.

I bet you are dying to find out what Jack Bauer has to do with the way you model your spiritual life for your kids, aren't you? Well, if you had been hanging around our home during the time when *24* was aired on television, it wouldn't have taken long for you to figure out that I'm a big fan. You'd hear me reference something from last week's show or ask my boys what they thought was going to happen next week. You'd hear me joke with my boys about any of our favorite Jack Bauer lines, such as, "I'm gonna need a hacksaw."* You'd see me put on a DVD of a previous season of *24* while I run on the treadmill after work.

In the same way, I want my boys to know that I'm excited about God and what Christ has done for me. I want them to hear it in my daily conversation. I want them to see it in the books I read and that we discuss together. I want them to hear my love for God in my voice when we pray together. I want them to experience how I look to God for wisdom and guidance when I have a problem. I want them to notice that I take time to read my Bible and have quiet devotional times. I want them to observe that when I fail, I ask for forgiveness and then set my sights on obeying God more faithfully. As they live with me each day, I want to be a living picture of a dad who is eternally thankful that Jesus died for him and delivered him from the chains of sin that were taking over his life. In other words, I want my words and actions to show my boys that I am infinitely more excited about Jesus Christ than about Jack Bauer.

My dad has left me with many such memories. I remember one occasion in California when he and my mother were having a difficult time in their marriage. I was an older teenager at the time, and my dad and I were sitting in the car one afternoon talking about the situation. I honestly thought they were going to get a divorce. However, my dad surprised me. While the look on his face and the exasperation in his

_____
*You don't want to know.

voice told me how difficult the current situation was, he said, "Todd, my faith is simple enough to believe that God can work this thing out, and I'm going to trust him." Last February, my dad and mom celebrated their fiftieth wedding anniversary.

My dad's example of an unwavering faith in God through many trials has given me a model to copy when I am faced with mountains that seem too high to climb. His life is a living picture for me that God is faithful to those who trust him and his arm is not too short to save nor his ear too dull to hear (see Isa. 59:1). My boys need to see that same living picture. Your kids do too.

Your Marriage

I am fortunate to have married well. This means that I have a great wife who is willing* to put up with the antics of her predominantly male household. I don't know about you, but I've got room to improve in some of the marriage areas—such as all of them. For instance, Lora has this strange notion that shoes should be kept in one particular spot in the house, a place she refers to as a closet. Now, this idea runs counter to my "hunter-gatherer" instinct that causes me to leave my shoes in approximately four different locations of the house at any given time to maximize accessibility, in case a wild elk should pass by and I would need to go get my friend David to come and kill it.

This type of situation is common in all marriages and is characterized by two things. The first is the husband having a practical and efficient idea, such as vacuuming only when dust particles are large enough to actually *see*. The second is the wife having an impractical and inefficient idea, such as asking the husband to help with housework during any of the three off-limits times: when he (1) is preparing to watch

*Usually, that is.

or (2) is in the act of watching or (3) has recently watched any type of sporting event.

The purpose of this chapter is not to prevent these situations from occurring; this is impossible. It is simply to point out that however you handle these situations, your kids will see it. If they are boys, you'll be showing them how to treat their future wife someday. If they are girls, you'll be showing them what they should expect from their future husband. The Bible tells husbands to "love your wives, just as Christ loved the church and gave himself up for her" (Eph. 5:25). So if you "love your wife" by putting your shoes away, your kids will know it. If you "love your wife" by talking with her about problems when they arise and finding a positive solution together, they'll notice that. If you don't, they'll notice that too. The point is, whatever you do, they're going to notice it, and that will be the model they will copy.

There are many other things your kids will notice about the way you treat your wife besides where you park your shoes. They'll notice that you make her feel important and loved. They'll notice that you kiss her and hold her hand. They'll notice how respectfully you talk to her. They'll see that you work out problems and disagreements together in a creative way. They'll notice that you watch the occasional "chick flick" together.* They'll *really* notice when you help with the laundry and dishes. They'll notice that you apologize to your wife instead of turning the tables and blaming her. They'll notice when they see you reading a marriage book together. They'll notice that you enjoy doing things with each other. They'll notice that your wife is truly your best friend.

Here's a final thought for those of you who have daughters. In *Strong Fathers, Strong Daughters*, Meg Meeker asks dads to picture their daughter on her wedding day and then take an imaginary look at the young man she is about to marry. Meeker asks, "If you could pick his personality, what would

---

*At least once every bicentennial year.

it be like?" Probably reading your mind, Meeker offers an answer to her own question: "You would want a young man totally committed and faithful to your daughter. You would want him to be hardworking, compassionate, honest, and courageous. You would want a man who will protect your daughter. You would want a man of integrity." Good answer. Then Meeker lowers the boom: "Before your daughter marries, you need to be that man." She explains, "The man you see at the other end of the aisle will undoubtedly be a reflection of you—be that good or bad. It's the way it is: women are drawn to what they know."[1]

Dads, your children are watching you all the time. They are watching your spiritual life and in so doing are learning how to apply their faith to their own daily lives. They are watching your marriage to see if you will "love your wife" by putting away your shoes. Even your daughter's eventual choice for a husband will be impacted by the kind of man she sees in you. You are the living picture that God has placed in their lives. Just as my friend David is showing his son how to hunt for elk, a great dad will show his kids what it looks like to love God and to love his wife. Showing them how to make a tasty leaf and bug salad is optional.

Key Points

1. Your children will learn many life-shaping lessons from you just by *watching*.
2. God has placed you in your kids' lives to be a living picture for them to learn from.
3. You model many things for your kids every day, including how you talk, listen, spend your time, value relationships, act respectfully, control your anger, and so on.
4. Your everyday spiritual life will give your kids a model for how to walk closely with God through thick and thin.

5. The way you treat your wife will show your kids what a healthy marriage looks like.

Getting to Work

1. You are a living picture that your kids watch every day. What is a positive behavior that you have tried to model for your kids? What is a negative behavior your kids have seen or heard from you?

2. Read 1 Corinthians 11:1; 1 Timothy 4:12; and Titus 2:7–8. Paul clearly understood the power of modeling, as he invited believers to follow his example and encouraged Christian leaders to set a good example for others. He also told fathers to bring their kids up in the training and instruction of the Lord (see Eph. 6:4). How does modeling help a father accomplish this? What happens when a father's daily example contradicts the way God wants us to live?

3. Someone once said that the best lessons are "caught" not "taught." Take a look at the table of contents for a quick review of the topics we have covered so far. What important lessons will your kids "catch" as you put these chapters into practice?

4. Name two ways that you model your spiritual life for your kids. What is one spiritual area you can model more consistently?

5. What big lessons do you want your son or daughter to learn about marriage by watching you? How can you use modeling to get those lessons across?

The Friendship Factor

Young John Connor would have to choose his friends wisely. Connor had been raised by a mother who thought that a nuclear holocaust was imminent and that Skynet (the artificial intelligence computer program that would soon become more powerful than Starbucks) had targeted her for destruction by sending a "Terminator" (who looked strangely like the governor of California) from the future to kill her. This was all so that her son, the ever-so-lucky John Connor, who would go on to lead the Resistance and ultimately defeat Skynet in the future, would not be born. Are you following this? Because it gets better.

With his mother having been understandably locked up in the nearest psychiatric hospital, John was living with foster parents.* One afternoon, having turned into a high-tech ju-

---

*If you've seen the movie, you know this ultimately didn't work out too well for them.

venile delinquent, John was riding his motorcycle through the streets of his LA suburb, enjoying his new hobby of stealing money from ATM machines. However, little did he know that Skynet had secretly sent a super-duper Terminator, made of liquid metal that could take on the shape of any life form (obviously politicians and IRS agents were safe), back through time in order to kill him once and for all. This meant that any of his friends or relatives, or even a trusted police officer, could be the Terminator in disguise.

Here's where it gets weird. Not to be outdone, the future John Connor sent back an old-style Terminator (the Resistance had a smaller budget) to protect the past John Connor from this super-duper Terminator. Of course, the Terminator sent to protect him was the exact same model as the one that had been sent to kill his mother a few years earlier (and they say there are no good movies anymore). If mankind and the Resistance were to ultimately prevail against the machines, John would need to make some very careful choices about who his friends would be that day.

The Friendship Need

I can only hope that none of your kids will find themselves in the position that John Connor did in *Terminator 2*, although I would encourage you to keep an eye on Starbucks' computer system. However, while your kids probably won't have Terminators hunting them down, the choices they make about friends will have an equally important, future-changing impact.

A little-known scientific study recently discovered something that shocked the medical community: kids closely resemble actual human life. And like real people, kids want to be accepted. They want to fit in. Because you are becoming a great dad, I will assume that your kids already know how loved and accepted they are by you. But as they get older, your love and acceptance isn't enough; they want to be loved and accepted by other life-forms in the outside world. And not just any life-form in the outside world: your kids don't particularly care if they are accepted by the UPS driver. They want to be accepted by their peers. And this means making friends.

Now, making friends is a good thing. In fact, this is a process ordained by none other than God himself, who made us relationship-oriented creatures. It is in the arena of peer relationships that your kids will learn how to get along with other people, handle peer pressure, and actually talk with members of the opposite sex. In the ups and downs of making friends, your kids will learn who they are, who they are not, and what kind of person they want to be.

The Friendship Danger

As a dad, I began to feel my ability to safely cocoon my kids from the dangers of the outside world slipping through my fingers the day they started going to kindergarten and were exposed to other kids whose parents have probably been in psychiatric wards for thinking that they have been chased by Terminators sent from the future. No longer was I able to control every facet of their lives, as I did when they were younger.* Each day as they left for school, I knew that *today* was the day that the following exchange could take place:

My kid: "Hi Johnny, do you want to play catch?"
Johnny: "Sure, but first let's smoke pot and then go push over some old people."
My kid: "Okay."

As my boys have grown older, I have realized that I cannot choose their friends for them. Not to say that I haven't tried. Friendship choices can be influenced by a lot of things, not the least of which is the random mix of children that hap-

---

*The prenatal stage was the easiest.

pen to live in your neighborhood, attend your kids' school, and share their activities. So while you may need to put your foot down now and then ("No, Abby, you cannot date a drug dealer, even if he is cute."), I find it more helpful to think of how a great dad can *guide* his kids in their choice of friends. To that end, here is a way of talking about friends that I have used with my boys that has given them a helpful framework for making good friendship choices and us a helpful framework for talking about it.

The Friendship Circles

When you look at Jesus's life, it seems that he spent time with two basic groups of people: his disciples and everyone else. Being one who enjoys seizing every opportunity to draw an illustration on a dry erase board, this caused me to pick up my markers and draw two circles, one inside the other. While 99 percent of people in the law enforcement community taking an inkblot test would identify this shape as a donut, I called these friendship circles, with the smaller circle being the inner circle and the larger one being the outer circle.

The Inner Circle

Jesus had an inner circle. He spent most of his time with a hand-picked group of twelve close friends. Rumor has it that they went undefeated for several years at Torah Trivia night at the Nazareth synagogue.* However, the key point here is that Jesus's inner circle was not chosen at random; he was purposeful about who he invited into it. The Bible tells us that the choices we (and our kids) make about friends are extremely important. Take a look:

A righteous man is cautious in friendship, but the way of the wicked leads them astray. (Prov. 12:26)

*How would you like to be in a trivia contest against God?

He who walks with the wise grows wise, but a companion of fools suffers harm. (Prov. 13:20)

Do not make friends with a hot-tempered man, do not associate with one easily angered, or you may learn his ways and get yourself ensnared. (Prov. 22:24–25)

Do not envy wicked men, do not desire their company; for their hearts plot violence, and their lips talk about making trouble. (Prov. 24:1–2)

Everyone needs a quality inner circle of friends, and your kids are no exception. Where would Batman be without Alfred? Where would Robin Hood be without Little John? Where would SpongeBob be without Patrick and Squidward? Inner circle friends are the friends your kids will spend the most time with and who will have the most influence on their choices, view of themselves, and view of the world. Inner circle friends are powerful: they can strengthen your kids' faith and character, or they can weaken them.

A great dad will communicate this message: *choose your inner circle friends carefully*. If your kids are trying to walk on God's path for their lives, it is important that they be on the lookout for inner circle friends who share this commitment to Christ and are trying to stay on God's path themselves. Regular involvement in church youth activities is one great way to help your kids build these valuable relationships.

In addition to developing strong Christian friends, your child will naturally also develop some inner circle friends from school or activities who are not Christians (but are still great kids). Either way, while no kid will be perfect (not even yours), your kids should be thoughtful about who they invite into their inner circles. The bottom line is that whether Christian or not, inner circle friends should be kids who are developing positive character traits (e.g., honesty, loyalty, respectfulness, self-control, kindness) and are making good choices in the big areas: home, school, friends, language, drugs/alcohol, and the opposite sex.

Your kids' inner circle of friends will undoubtedly change over time. I have seen both my boys' inner circles change as they have moved from elementary school through middle school and into high school. A few good friends have been in their inner circles the whole time, while others have come along more recently. Both my boys have been in each other's inner circles as well.* Sometimes their inner circles have contained only one or two kids; other times there have been four or five. But inner circle friends will have an influence, and because of that, God tells us to choose them with wisdom and caution.

To help you discuss the importance of the inner circle with your kids, here are several discussion questions you can use (after drawing the friendship circles) to get started:

Inner Circle Discussion Questions

1. Why is your inner circle (closest friends) so important?
2. What kind of people does God want you to have in your inner circle?
3. How will having the right people in your inner circle help you to make wise decisions for your life?
4. How will having the wrong people in your inner circle hurt you?
5. Who do you know right now that might be a good inner circle friend?

The Outer Circle

The outer circle is rather large because it includes everyone your kids know who is not in their inner circle, including their friends on Facebook, Twitter, and Xbox Live. Some will be Christians; some won't. Some will have good inten-

*Some pet lovers think that dogs should be allowed in a child's inner circle, and this is acceptable. But no cats.

tions; some won't. Some will know how to hot-wire a car; some won't.

Either way, God has a lot to say about how he wants your kids to interact with their outer circle. Take a look:

You are the light of the world—like a city on a mountain, glowing in the night for all to see. Don't hide your light under a basket! Instead, put it on a stand and let it shine for all. In the same way, let your good deeds shine out for all to see, so that everyone will praise your heavenly father. (Matt. 5:14–16 NLT)

For God was in Christ, reconciling the world to himself, no longer counting people's sins against them. This is the wonderful message he has given us to tell others. (2 Cor. 5:19 NLT)

Dear friends, I urge you, as aliens and strangers in the world, to abstain from sinful desires, which war against your soul. Live such good lives among the pagans that, though they accuse you of doing wrong, they may see your good deeds and glorify God on the day he visits us. (1 Peter 2:11–12)

Again we see God's friendship plan in the life of Jesus. He had a carefully chosen inner circle with whom he spent most of his time, but he also spent time with lots of different people, as do your kids when they go to school, participate in sports and clubs, or engage in community service.* In fact, Jesus was even criticized by the Pharisees for the time he spent with tax collectors and sinners.

But when Jesus was with his outer circle, he was there for one purpose: "Jesus said, 'It is not the healthy who need a doctor, but the sick'" (Matt. 9:12). He was there to be salt and light, to tell and show his outer circle friends about his Father. He was there not to be influenced by them but to influence them. Here are a few ideas for how your kids can have the right impact on their outer circle friends:

*Hopefully not court-ordered.

1. *Be friendly*—While not everyone in your child's outer circle will always display the greatest behavior or language (for example, they may drop a fake mouse in the lap of an unsuspecting teacher), being friendly and respectful to everyone at school and other activities is how God wants us to interact with others (see 1 Peter 2:17) and opens doors for other positive interactions down the road.

2. *Be encouraging*—Showing encouragement to those around us communicates caring and interest in their lives. Whether during a game of basketball or after taking a hard test, when your kids offer an encouraging word to their outer circle friends, they are showing God's love in a tangible way.

3. *Be a positive influence*—Matthew 5:14–16 and 1 Peter 2:11–12 make it clear that God wants us to live lives that honor him and reflect his love and character. Paul tells us to "Be imitators of God, therefore, as dearly loved children and live a life of love, just as Christ loved us" (Eph. 5:1–2). How can your child be a positive influence to his or her outer circle friends? Here are a few ways that make a big impact:
   - Dressing modestly
   - Telling only clean jokes
   - Using appropriate language
   - Showing discretion and accepting parental guidance in the movies they watch and music they listen to
   - Respectfully standing up for others who are teased or bullied
   - Being honest
   - Being a good sport
   - Making their best effort at school and activities

4. *Set clear boundaries*—There will be times when your kids will need to set clear boundaries, which may be different than the boundaries that some of their friends will choose. This is an extremely important topic to

discuss with your children and revisit over time, both individually and in your family times. Boundary issues when your kids are in second grade (e.g., whether or not to sing the "Barney Song" with new-fangled lyrics) will be quite different from the boundary issues in high school, but they are all equally important in your children developing the ability to internally and externally say no to peer pressure.

Important boundary areas for discussion include language, honesty, media choices, clothing styles, teasing/bullying, involvement with the opposite gender, social gatherings, and substance use. In fact, since you are a coach, I would encourage you to actually do role-play practices with your kids for how to uphold their boundaries (in a friendly and respectful way) in difficult boundary situations, such as when friends at a sleepover invite him to play a video game that he knows he is not allowed to play, or when several of your child's friends are making fun of another kid behind their back.

Paul reminded us, "Whatever you do, whether in word or deed, do it all in the name of the Lord Jesus" (Col. 3:17). As your children choose to obey God by learning to set clear boundaries and stand up to the social temptations that will most certainly come their way, they will experience the blessings God has promised to those who stay on the safety of his path. And a great dad will be sure to point that out.

5. *Look for opportunities*—Finally, your kids should always be watching for opportunities in which their faith can impact their outer circle friendships. It may be telling a friend with a sick parent that she will be praying for them, or inviting a few kids to a fun church youth group activity. Other times, your child may have an opportunity to tell someone why she believes in God or how knowing God has impacted her life. Peter tells us to "Always be prepared to give an answer to everyone

who asks you to give the reason for the hope that you have. But do this with gentleness and respect" (1 Peter 3:15). This can be another great topic for family time discussions as you help your kids learn appropriate ways to live out and share their faith.

Below are five discussion questions you can use as you discuss the importance of how your kids interact with their outer circle:

Outer Circle Discussion Questions

1. Who is in your outer circle?
2. Does God want you to be influenced by your outer circle of friends, or does he want you to influence them? What did Jesus do with his outer circle friends?
3. Read the five ideas for impacting your outer circle friends listed above (you can shorten and paraphrase as needed). Do you think these areas are important? Why? Which areas are you doing well in? Which ones can you improve in?
4. What kind of influence do you want to have on your outer circle friends? How can you have this kind of influence?
5. What are the names of three people in your outer circle whom you can pray for and look for opportunities to influence toward God?

The Friendship Result

Your kids are going to have friendships. They are going to have inner and outer circles that will change over time. However, the choices they make about who they invite into their inner circle and how they act with both their inner and outer circle friends will make all the difference. If they choose inner circle friends who make good choices and who will strengthen their walk with God, and if they do their best to be salt and light with their outer circle friends, friendships can be a source of great joy and blessing. With your guidance, your kids will learn valuable lessons about the importance of staying on God's path that will prepare them for the friendship challenges they will face as they get older.

The friendship choices your kids make with their inner and outer circles will have a big impact on their present and future. To borrow a concept from chapter 5, this is *big stuff*, and a great dad will be sure to talk about it with his kids often. In fact, when you are wrapping up a discussion about friends, let your kids know that you'll be checking in with them again soon by putting on some dark sunglasses, looking at them with your most emotionless Austrian face, and saying, "Aaa'll be baaack."

Key Points

1. God made us to have friends.
2. While you may need to protect your kids from negative friendship choices now and then, your main goal is to guide them in choosing the right friends.
3. Inner circle friends should include kids who make good choices in the big areas and who will strengthen your kids' walk with God.
4. God wants us to influence our outer circle friends rather than be influenced by them.
5. Making wise choices with friends will help your kids experience the blessing of staying on God's path.

Getting to Work

1. Think about your own friends for a minute. Who is a good inner circle friend who helps you stay on God's path? What is it about that friend that you appreciate? Have you ever had a friend who influenced you away from God's path?

2. What role should a dad play in influencing his kids' friendship choices? How can you balance being protective with teaching your kids how to make the right choices?
3. Read again the verses from Proverbs provided on pages 189–90. Why do you think inner circle friendship choices are so important? What kind of choices have your kids made with their inner circles?
4. Read again the three passages provided on page 192. What do they tell us about the way we should interact with our outer circle friends? How are your kids doing at being influencers rather than being influenced by their outer circle?
5. Make it a point to introduce your kids to the friendship circles, either one-on-one or in your next family time discussion. Use the Bible verses provided and the inner and outer circle discussion questions to start your kids thinking about their friendship choices. Make sure that you come back to this topic regularly, as friendship issues will always be an important part of your children's lives. Your kids will thank you for being a dad who cares enough to help them learn to make wise friendship choices so they can experience the blessings of loving God and loving others.

Draw the Line

Research has shown that dads like quizzes.* In fact, many bestselling books contain quizzes, so in a cheap attempt to make this a bestselling book, here's a quiz: Where would you draw the line?

1. Your child wants to play a violent video game. You should:
   a. Tell him that Jesus did not play violent video games so neither can he.
   b. Tell him to go ahead, but make sure you don't leave any loaded guns around the house.
   c. Tell him the game is okay as long as he is not hurting any plants or animals.
2. Your child develops a strong inclination toward "gansta rap" music. You should:

*I asked a couple guys.

a. Secretly replace all music on his iPod with the Gaither Vocal Band.

b. Tell him that he can listen to any rap music that contains no swearing, vulgarity, or negative references to women. Problem solved.

c. Inform him that "gansta rap" has coincidentally become your favorite music also. Immediately begin turning your baseball cap sideways, put a fake "grill" on your teeth, and repeatedly ask him, "Wat up?" Do this at school functions and whenever his friends come to visit.

3. Your child would rather play video games than interact with other members of the human race. You should:

a. Tell him that you don't like the human race either, and as a result, you will be his new video game partner. This means that he will have to play games that Dad is able to understand, which limits the choices to Pac-Man and Galactica.

b. Only buy video games in a foreign language, which will make playing the video games educational and thus repel him.

c. Tell him that for each hour of video game time, he must watch one hour of *Dancing with the Stars*.

To Draw or Not to Draw

In each of the above situations, which touch on the topics of video game content, music content, and time spent engaged in electronic activities, you drew a line. Make no mistake about it: a great dad is a line-drawing dad. This is especially important when it comes to electronic activities.

What kind of electronic activities? Video games. Television. Computer games. Movies. Music. The internet. These are sources for lots of fun, positive, and even highly educational activities, such as games that let you race a souped-up porta-potty for hours on end or where you become a member of the criminal underground and do all the things needed to get ahead in that world, such as steal, kill, and refuse to pay your parking tickets.

As a dad, I know what you are thinking: *Where do I find great games like that?* Before you get too excited, let me remind you that the creators of many of the games, songs, and movies that our kids want to play, listen to, and watch probably don't share your personal value system. Big surprise, I know. However, the value system they do have comes through loud and clear, and its impact on your kids' thinking should not be underestimated. Under our noses, a worldview that says anything and everything is okay is being pumped into our kids through the electronic media faster than steroids into major league baseball players.

Sometimes the danger is not just in *what* our kids are watching, playing, or listening to but in *how much time* they spend in those activities. According to a recent report from the Kaiser Family Foundation, kids between the ages of eight and eighteen spend an average of over four hours a day watching television and an additional two and a half hours a day playing computer or video games. And that doesn't count the average of two and a half hours each day they spend listening to music.[1] Even if your kids don't spend four to seven hours a day on electronic activities, the time they do spend reminds me of my daily calorie intake: it adds up quicker than you think.

Your kids need a dad who will draw the line to keep them safe from media danger. The danger of thinking that casual sex is harmless. The danger of thinking that bloody gore is cool or funny. The danger of spending more time with electronics than with real people. Dangers their young eyes and ears may not recognize, but very real dangers nonetheless. The Bible gives us a guideline for the kind of "stuff" that we should be putting into our brains: "Whatever is true, whatever is noble, whatever is right, whatever is pure, whatever is lovely, whatever is admirable—if anything is excellent or praiseworthy—think about such things" (Phil. 4:8).

In this chapter we will discuss three line-drawing topics every great dad needs to be on top of: when to draw the line, where to draw the line, and how to draw the line.

When to Draw the Line

When Jake was four years old, he enjoyed the typical collection of preschool television shows and videos, ranging from *Blue's Clues* to your typical Disney animation. However, one day Lora and I noticed that Jake's play had suddenly become more violent in nature. He would sit at his plastic picnic table in our family room and bang his little plastic horses into each other, saying, "Kill, kill," while making crashing sound effects to complete his 3-D play experience. In fact, when he played with almost any toy, he started to insert fighting and killing as his main play theme.

I'm not sure if Ted Bundy started out this way, but Jake's repetitive use of the word *kill* was clearly out of the ordinary, as it was one of the words that Lora and I were careful not to use in front of the kids, along with *maim, mutilate,* and *dismember*. Being fairly certain that *kill* was not the "word of the day" at preschool, Lora and I tried to think about where he had picked it up.

As we considered the possibilities, I wondered if he could have heard it on television or videos, although we thought this was highly unlikely because he was only allowed to watch shows that we had approved, and *The Godfather* hadn't yet been added to his approved movie list. However, as I examined the list of his most watched videos, which included favorites such as *Robin Hood, Pinocchio, Peter Pan,* and most recently, *Beauty and the Beast,* it hit me—"Kill the beast! Kill the beast!" Could this be where Jake was picking it up?

As a psychologist, every neuron in my brain screamed in unison: *Experiment!* So, from our video collection, I chose the five videos that I judged to have the most violence or aggression in them (including *Beauty and the Beast*) and secretly removed them from the video cupboard. Thankfully, Jake never noticed, and he was happy watching the remaining videos. The result? Within three weeks, Lora and I were delighted to find that the words "Kill, kill" and the aggressive play had vanished completely. I am still waiting to hear back from the Nobel Peace Prize people.

Thankfully for Jake, we drew the line; otherwise he'd undoubtedly still be chanting "Kill, kill" today, which might cause problems at school. I strongly encourage you to talk with your wife about *where* you both will draw the line regarding the type of electronic activities you allow and the amount of time you allow your kids to engage in them. We'll discuss these two areas in more detail in the next section. But make no doubt about it: no matter what your kids' ages, the answer to the question of *when* to start drawing the line is *now*.*

Where to Draw the Line

The two areas where lines need to be drawn include the *content* of the electronic activities and the *time* your kids are allowed to spend on them. Let's tackle both of those issues now.

1. **Content.** If you are waiting for me to tell you what you should or should not let your kids watch or listen to, then you'll be waiting a long time. That is your decision. My goal is to encourage you, together with your wife, to draw a line *somewhere* and to prayerfully consider where that should be.

To give you an example from our family, there have been many video games, movies, and musical selections that our kids were not allowed to play, watch, or listen to. Often these have included movies sprinkled with bad language, crude humor, or sexual content; television shows that contained humor or themes that we deemed inappropriate for our kids' ages; video or computer games that displayed graphic vio-

*If your child's first word was "TiVo," you may have waited too long.

lence; or any kind of music involving a banjo. I have found that we have changed where we draw the line as our boys have become older teens, but this is done on a case-by-case basis, and there are still plenty of movies, games, and musical artists that we all pass on. Lora and I usually agree where to draw the line, and when we don't, we follow the one whose conscience is on the safer side.

I can't think of a time when I regretted drawing a line to protect my boys from inappropriate material entering their brains. I can remember a few times when I regretted that I didn't. That's part of a great dad's job: to see danger your kids don't see and to love them enough to protect them from it. You are not drawing a line because it sounds like a fun way to flex your parental muscles. When you draw a line, you are showing your kids that the Bible is not a book of nice ideas but is God's guidance as to what is truly healthy and what is not. Unlike the messages that permeate the electronic entertainment industry, you're showing your kids that some things are right and some things are wrong. If they don't get that message from you, they probably won't get it at all.

2. *Time.* A concept that I have found to be very helpful in deciding how much time kids should be engaged in electronic activities is *balance*. Even if the content of their music, television and movie choices, and video and computer games is outstanding, balance can still be an issue. Just like you can have too much of anything (except horsepower and power tools, of course), your kids can have too much electronic time, and that will put them, and your family, out of balance.

Your kids have lots of important things they need to be doing: homework; helping out around the house; playing with friends; reading; family activities; participating in sports, clubs, or hobbies; possibly practicing an instrument; and of course, electronic play is fine also. When your child is involved in a balanced selection of healthy activities, electronics are usually not a problem. When electronic activities get out of balance and start to steal time from the other important areas, that's when the problems occur.

There are many different ways to keep the time spent on electronic activities in balance. Some families have very limited electronics on school days. Other parents just use the simple guideline of making sure that homework and other assigned tasks are done before any electronics can be used and even then require their kids to have fun in non-electronic ways as well. You might consider just doing away with electricity altogether. However you choose to do it, it is important that you listen to your internal "balance-o-meter" and make sure that you don't let electronics crowd out the more important things, such as *Monday Night Football*.

How to Draw the Line

The fact that you have read this far in this book tells me something about you: you suffer from insomnia. But to reward your effort, let me give you a couple tips on *how* to draw the line with your kids. The answer to "how" really comes from the "why." Why do you draw the line for your kids? The first answer is that you want to protect their minds from dangerous material and keep them from getting out of balance. The second answer is that you want them to learn how to draw the line for themselves someday.

If you want your kids to learn to draw the line for themselves, then *how* you draw the line becomes very important. If you draw the line as King Henry VIII might have ("Because I said so! Now, off with your head!"), then your kids will probably respect your line-drawing boundaries until the second you turn your back. The reason for this is that your line-drawing decisions will seem like irrelevant, "old school" rules that are being forced on them instead of discussed *with* them. They will know *where* you are drawing the line, but they won't understand *why*.

Here are a few ideas that might help. When your kids are younger, drawing the line is fairly simple: you just allow them to engage in electronic activities that you think are appropriate, and that's it. If they ask why they can't watch a certain show or play a certain game, you just tell them that the show or game in question is inappropriate and briefly explain why. Kind of like how your wife tells you what not to wear.

As your kids get older, however, the best way to draw the line is to talk about it. You will undoubtedly revisit these discussions from time to time as your kids get older and become interested in different types of electronic activities, such as online gambling. You will probably adjust where you draw certain lines as your kids get older as well. The topic of how to enjoy electronic activities in a way that pleases God is a great topic for both one-on-one and family time discussions.

It is always good to begin these discussions by listening to your kids' opinions and letting them unload their truck. Once they have shared their ideas, they will be more open to hearing your thoughts about the benefits and potential dangers that electronics can bring to them or to your family. This is a great time to take a look at a few Bible verses together that touch on this topic (see the Getting to Work questions). You want your kids to understand that the lines you draw are like safety rails that help keep them safe from real dangers and slippery slopes that can pull them (or anyone) off of God's path. As a loving dad, you want your kids to enjoy the benefits of electronic media while remembering to engage in *every* activity in a way that pleases God (see Col. 3:17).

It won't take very many discussions for your kids to get the idea of where you draw the line. Bottom line, if you think a certain electronic activity is inappropriate or that it has become out of balance, then that is when and where you will warmly and respectfully draw the line. Chances are high that your kids are already quite aware that a certain electronic activity crosses the line; they were just curious to see if you would let it slide. Somewhere, hidden deep inside (perhaps *very* deep), they are glad that you love them enough to draw the line, even if they temporarily turn into Attila the Hun when the line gets drawn.

You are helping your kids begin to think about how they apply God's Word to their entertainment choices. You are teaching them that there actually *are* unhealthy forms of entertainment and showing them how to say no when the entertainment starts to lead them down the wrong path. They may temporarily think that you are not a fun dad. But with the perspective that comes with age, they'll realize that you cared enough to be a great dad.

Key Points

1. A great dad is a line-drawing dad.
2. Line drawing begins as soon as your kids are old enough to sit in front of a television.
3. Drawing the line will protect your kids from inappropriate content and the relativistic messages that come along with it.
4. Electronic activities can be a great source of fun as long as they are kept in balance.
5. Discussing where to draw the line on electronics, both individually and as a family, will help your kids learn to draw the line for themselves.

Getting to Work

1. As dads, we don't only draw lines for our kids; we also draw lines for ourselves. Where do you draw the line for the content (e.g., language, violence, sexual themes) and time spent engaged in electronic activities? Do you need to reconsider where you draw the line for yourself?
2. What are some of the dangerous messages that kids can pick up from electronics? How can those messages subtly influence their behavior and choices?

3. Read Philippians 4:8; Colossians 3:16–17; and 1 John 2:15–17. What do these passages suggest about the type of content that God wants us to put into our minds? How does this apply to electronics?
4. How well do your kids show balance with the time they spend involved in electronic activities? Are there any important activities that are getting left behind? How can you help your child restore a healthy balance?
5. Do you need to have a discussion with one of your kids, or together as a family, about where to draw the line? If so, here are some questions that will help get your discussion started:
   a. "What do you think about _____ (playing video games, watching movies, listening to music)?"
   b. "Tell me some ways that _____ can be a good thing for you. How about for our family?"
   c. "Is there any way that _____ could be bad for you? Or for our family?"
   d. "What does the Bible say about what we should watch, play, or listen to?"
   e. "Why is it important to keep electronic activities in balance?"
   f. "What can you say/do when your friends are allowed to watch/play/listen to something that you're not?"

Wanted: Great Dads

(Superheroes Need Not Apply)

Many of you have seen the animated movie *Toy Story*, and I bet you found an unexplainable place of affection in your heart for little Andy's favorite space hero, Buzz Lightyear, didn't you? As my last death-defying feat of amazement in this book, I will now reveal the mystery of why *every* dad who has ever seen this movie felt this otherworldly kinship with the lovable space ranger.

When we first met Buzz as Andy's favorite new birthday present, we quickly discovered that Buzz truly believed he was a *real* space ranger whose spacecraft had malfunctioned and crashed on planet Earth. Oblivious to evidence to the contrary and despite Woody's insistence that Buzz was actually a toy, Buzz was absolutely convinced that he could fly, fire a laser beam, and ultimately return to Space Command and save the universe from the evil Emperor Zurg.

As the movie unfolded, an unfortunate series of events caused Buzz and Woody to end up as captives in the house of Sid, Andy's twisted next-door neighbor, who loved interrogating his toys and then strapping them to explosives when they refused to talk. As they were trying to escape, Buzz happened to see a television commercial for a Buzz Lightyear action figure with all the same features that he possessed. All at once, it hit him like a meteor: Woody was right; *he really was only a toy.* Buzz was devastated by the realization that he was not a superhero after all. With his purpose for living suddenly evaporated into thin air, a depressed and dejected Buzz didn't even lift a plastic finger to escape when Sid taped him to an explosive rocket that he planned to detonate the next morning.

You might remember the scene where Buzz was taped to the rocket on Sid's desk and Woody was trapped underneath an old plastic milk crate, unable to free himself. Sid was asleep, and this was their last chance to escape. Woody was trying to get Buzz to help them escape, but Buzz could see no reason to go on.

Buzz: "You were right all along. I'm not a space ranger, I'm just a toy—a stupid, little, insignificant toy."

Woody: "Whoa, hey, wait a minute. Being a toy is a lot better than being a space ranger."

Buzz: "Yeah right."

Woody: "No, it is. Look, over in that house is a kid who thinks you are the greatest. And it's not because you are a space ranger, pal, it's because you're a toy. You are *his* toy."

Buzz pondered Woody's words for a moment and looked down at Andy's name written in permanent marker on the bottom of his foot. Woody was right. It was Buzz Lightyear *the toy* that Andy loved. As this truth penetrated his space helmet and sank into his plastic head, Buzz came back to life, filled with an even stronger sense of meaning and purpose: Andy loved him, and he didn't have to be a superhero to love and protect his boy. He could do it just the way he was.

My Name Is Buzz

So what is the connection that we felt with Buzz? Simple. Every dad is a Buzz Lightyear. For a while, our kids think we have superhuman strength and can pull quarters out of their ears. But we know better. While our kids look up to us as superheroes of sorts, we know that we are fallen and flawed and filled with more mistakes than they will ever know. We know exactly how Buzz felt when he saw that television commercial, because we have had that same feeling hundreds of times. But Woody's words of encouragement to Buzz apply equally to us. Let me change a few words in Woody's last sentence, and I want you to picture him talking right to you: "Look, over in that house is a kid who thinks you are the greatest. And it's not because you are a superhero, pal. It's because you're a dad. You are *his* dad."

You have just spent several hours reading* through nineteen chapters about becoming a great dad. You know that a great dad looks for the gold in his kids, communicates respectfully, stays connected, teaches valuable lessons, and leads through his example. That's what a great dad does. But let me remind you of something a great dad is not. As I mentioned in the introduction, a great dad is not a perfect dad. Good thing too, or none of us would have a chance. A great dad is an *authentic* dad—a dad who does his best to follow God and teaches his kids to do the same. But that dad will not be without sins and mistakes, so I have to figure that God wants us to show our kids how to handle those too. Listen to how John Eldredge puts it in his book *You Have What It Takes*:

*Perhaps dozing would be a more accurate term.

210

I know that I have blown it with my sons. More times than I want to admit. I know that I have hurt them and will hurt them again before this whole thing is over. I am a man "under construction" undergoing renovation, and sometimes the uglier parts of me slip out. Jesus is not finished with me yet. I will never be the perfect dad. But here is what I am counting on: Love covers over a multitude of sins (1 Peter 4:8). I really want to do a great job as a dad. But I know I will not do it perfectly. Sometimes I'm just too tired to offer what they need; other times I'm just plain selfish. So this verse is what I'm banking on, more than anything else as a father.[1]

Eldredge is right; love does cover a multitude of sins, and we can all be thankful that it does. But there is something else that we can bank on too. Remember, you are not completing your Project Dad on your own. In fact, it is not even *your* project: it is God's project, and he's not known for being a quitter (just ask Pharaoh). Remember Paul's encouragement in Philippians 1:6: "He who began a good work in you will carry it on to completion until the day of Christ Jesus." If you have children (which I'm assuming you do, or are planning to—otherwise you went to the wrong book section), then God intends for you to have an awesome, life-influencing impact on your children. And as the twenty-first-century spokesman for dads, Larry the Cable Guy, would say, God will help you "Git 'er done."

Maybe you're thinking, *But Todd, you don't know how many mistakes I've made*, or *You don't know how my father treated me*, or perhaps, *I never even knew my dad*. I want you to slowly put the remote down, back away from your bag of BBQ chips, and remember two things: (1) making mistakes just means that you are an imperfect dad like the rest of us, and (2) having a bad or absent father won't *make* you a bad father any more than having a good father will *make* you a good one. Not every alcoholic had an alcoholic dad, and not every child with an alcoholic father turns into an alcoholic. One of my close friends is an awesome dad, and he never even knew his own father. In fact, he was raised by his mother and grandmother.* Of course it helps to have a good role model as a dad (that's what *you* are going to be for your kids), but your life and decisions are not ruled by what has happened in your past. God has placed one person and one person alone in charge of your choices, and that person is holding this book right now.

The First Step

One night I stayed up late after work; Lora had already gone to bed. I fixed myself a peanut butter sandwich and flipped on the television, hoping to find something interesting to watch. I skipped around the channels until I happened onto a late-night talk show where the theme was "Stop Piercing and Tattooing Yourself." After watching a few minutes of this, I felt the sudden urge to turn the television off and pray for my two boys, who were two and four at the time and, thankfully, still tattooless.

With the images of massive quantities of metal and ink forced into the human body still fresh in my mind, I prayed with a sense of urgency, "God, Jake and Luke will soon be going to school. They're going to be exposed to all sorts of things I can't control: all sorts of kids, all sorts of music, all sorts of influences that can take them away from you. Please be with them. Please watch over them. Please keep them safe. Please help me to be the kind of parent that will teach them to value you." All of a sudden, I felt as though God inaudibly spoke to my heart and said, "Then *you* value me."

I thought to myself, *What does that mean? How do I value God? Do I value God?* Sitting at the kitchen table, I took inventory of the amount of time I spent in prayer, the focus of my discussions, how I responded to crises and hard times, the amount of time I spent reading the Bible, the amount of

*He is also very good at baking pies.

times discussion of God was a natural part of my everyday language, the amount of time I prayed with my kids, my decisions, my priorities, my personal obedience. I immediately felt convicted and realized that I didn't value God as he deserves. Right there, I asked God to forgive me and to help me become a dad who values him the way I should.

That is the first step: realizing that we are utterly dependent on God to help us become what he has created us to be; acknowledging our sins and failings in how we think, talk, connect, act, and lead; and laying them at the cross of Christ, where he is always ready to accept and forgive those who ask. I took that step many years ago and have taken it countless times since. As the apostle John reminded us, "If we claim to be without sin, we deceive ourselves and the truth is not in us. If we confess our sins, he is faithful and just and will forgive us our sins and purify us from all unrighteousness" (1 John 1:8–9). In fact, I believe that a great dad takes this step every day. You won't become the dad God made you to be without it. And it is the first step that makes the second step possible.

The Second Step

The Tennessee Titans' head coach, Jeff Fisher, knows a thing or two about the second step. The second step is getting to work at making your dreams a reality by making the most of your strengths and working on your weaknesses until they also become strengths. In Christian Klemash's book *How to Succeed in the Game of Life*, here's Fisher's advice on working toward your dreams:

> I would emphasize how important it is to work on your weaknesses every single day. We all have been given strengths, but we have to work on the weaknesses and turn them into strengths in order to realize our potential. That player who is a great intermediate receiver and averages six to eight catches

a game on the intermediate routes, yet lacks the ability to go downfield—every day he needs to work on his downfield skills because he already has the intermediate skills. You must work on the weaknesses every day.[2]

Do you remember that thought I dropped into your brain in the introduction? In case your memory is like mine, here it is again: *God made me to be a great dad.* That is not science fiction; that is a fact. God did not make you to be a superhero; otherwise he would have given you the ability to understand the need for a dust ruffle.* He made you to be a great dad, and luckily for you, that's just what your kids need. So once you have acknowledged your failings and your need for God's help, then it's time to lock 'n' load and get to work.

Will Rogers astutely observed, "Even though you are on the right track, you will get run over if you just sit there."[3] Below is a list of many of the great dad characteristics you have learned in this book. Some of these characteristics are already becoming a regular part of your life. Others are skills you still need to work on. Take a look:

Great Dad Characteristics

Knows the details of each of his kids' lives	Searches for the special "prizes" inside each of his kids
Looks for the gold	Seizes every opportunity to make an impact
Turns mistakes into lessons	Points out positive choices, attributes, and results
Avoids communication potholes	Talks about little and big things
Develops a warm communication style	Uses I-statements
Uses positive attention to improve kids' behavior	Connects with body language
Spends regular time with kids	Treats family respectfully

*The fact that many of you do not even know what a dust ruffle is simply underscores my point.

Builds and protects relationship bridge	Is a good listener
Has a regular family time	Acts like a coach instead of a referee
Controls his anger	Teaches kids how to positively think and respond
Teaches kids how to approach problems creatively	Uses dad flexible thoughts
Has a warm and loving discipline style	Uses discipline to teach the right lessons the right way
Loves his wife for his kids to see	Sets an example with his spiritual life
Guides kids in friendship choices	Draws the line with electronics
Helps kids learn to draw the line for themselves	Recognizes his need for God's help in becoming a great dad

If you're serious about wanting to be a great dad, I want you to do three things right now. Take your time and do them slowly and thoughtfully. First, take a pencil and draw a circle around the traits you have already begun to improve at or that were already strong for you to begin with. Each time you circle a trait, thank God for his faithfulness by praying, "Lord, thank you for helping me to grow in this area. Please help me to grow even stronger."

Second, I want you to draw a double circle around the traits you want to develop even more as you grow into the father God desires you to be. These are the traits that you need to work on the most. As you draw each double circle, commit that trait to God by praying, "Lord, I ask you to build this characteristic in me. I will do whatever you ask me to do in order for this trait to grow in my life."

Third, read through the traits you have double circled one more time. Then close your eyes and imagine yourself exhibiting those traits. See yourself handling a discipline situation with patience and wisdom. Imagine yourself squeezing your child on the knee and telling her how much you love her. Picture yourself teaching your children about God during a family time. Soak in the look on your child's face as you become a coach who will listen to him when he is frustrated instead of shout at him because he has inconvenienced you.

How do you like the father that God is building? How will becoming that father impact your children and your family? "'For I know the plans I have for you,' declares the Lord, 'plans to prosper you and not to harm you, plans to give you hope and a future'" (Jer. 29:11). God is serious about you becoming a great dad to the gold nuggets he has given you, and he is in it for the long haul. The question is, are you?

Buzz Lightyear went on to have many great adventures, and last I heard, the evil Emperor Zurg has not taken over the galaxy. God has many wonderful adventures in store for you and your family. There will be trials and hardships along the way as well. But God has given your kids a great dad to help lead the way through them. As you allow God to shape the way you think, talk, connect, act, and lead your kids, he will use you to impact your kids and family not just for this life but for the one to come—or in the words of our favorite space ranger, "To infinity and beyond!"

Key Points

1. Every dad wants to be a superhero to his kids.
2. Every dad knows that he is a sinful and imperfect dad.
3. The first step for becoming a great dad is acknowledging your need for God's help.
4. The second step for becoming a great dad is getting to work on turning your weaknesses into strengths.
5. God is serious about you becoming a great dad. Are you?

Getting to Work

1. If you could have superpowers, which ones would you choose? (But ix-nay on the X-ray vision.)

2. Think of some of the areas where you've blown it as a dad. Some might be small; others might be big. Now read Psalm 51; Isaiah 1:16–18; and 1 John 1:8–9. As you confess your sins to God and seek to obey him with all your heart, what is his promised response?

3. The first step in becoming a great dad is acknowledging your need for God's help. If you haven't already, take a few minutes right now to confess your areas of sin and struggle to God and ask him to forgive you and to shape you into the person and dad that he wants you to be.

4. The second step in becoming a great dad is to get to work on your areas of weakness. Choose three of the Great Dad Characteristics you double circled on the list on pages 214–15. List two action steps you will take to get to work on each of these characteristics:

   Great Dad Characteristic #1: _____
   Action Step #1: _____
   Action Step #2: _____

   Great Dad Characteristic #2: _____
   Action Step #1: _____
   Action Step #2: _____

   Great Dad Characteristic #3: _____
   Action Step #1: _____
   Action Step #2: _____

5. Take a minute to reflect on what you have learned as you have read this book. Which lessons, stories, or analogies had the most impact on you? What changes have

you already put into place that will bring life-changing results for you and your family? Remember, your Project Dad journey does not end with this book—it begins. Take the three Great Dad Characteristics that you listed in the previous question and imagine yourself displaying those characteristics six months from now. How will those Great Dad Characteristics impact your kids and family? Do you like the dad God is building? I bet your kids do.

Notes

Introduction The Opportunity of a Lifetime

1. Lowell Streiker, *An Encyclopedia of Humor* (Peabody, MA: Hendrickson Publishers, 1998), 147.

2. Suzanne Le Menestrel, Ph.D., "What Do Fathers Contribute to Children's Well-Being?" *Child Trends*, May 1999, http://www.childtrends.org/files/dadchild.pdf.

3. Tim Russert, *Wisdom of Our Fathers* (New York: Random House, 2006), 251.

Chapter 1 Who Are These Little People?

1. Kevin Leman, *What a Difference a Daddy Makes* (Nashville: Thomas Nelson, 2000), 146–47.

2. Ibid., 147.

3. Bill Cosby, *Fatherhood* (New York: Doubleday, 1986), 34.

Chapter 2 There's a Prize Inside

1. Steve Chandler, *100 Ways to Motivate Yourself* (Franklin Lakes: NJ: Career Press, 1996), 19–20.

Chapter 3 What Are You Looking For?

1. You can learn more about Fast Listening in my book *Respectful Kids* (Colorado Springs: NavPress, 2006). It's really quite good. You should pick it up.

2. Todd Cartmell, *The Parent Survival Guide* (Grand Rapids: Zondervan, 2001), 193–201.

3. Laurence Peter, *Peter's Quotations* (New York: Quill, 1977), 393.

Chapter 4 Every Day Makes an Impact

1. "Quotations by Author: Mark Twain," The Quotations Page, 2010, http://www.quotationspage.com/quotes/Mark_Twain/31.
2. Tim Elmore, *Nurturing the Leader within Your Child* (Nashville: Thomas Nelson, 2001), 133–44.
3. Ibid., 142.

Chapter 5 When Dad Talks, Who Listens?

1. Phil McGraw, *Family First* (New York: Free Press, 2004), 53.

Chapter 6 Send a Message

1. The series is written by Dave Pilkey (New York: Scholastic, Inc.) and is required reading if you have kids who like adventure.
2. "Quotations by Author: Mother Teresa," The Quotations Page, 2010, http://www.quotationspage.com/quotes/Mother_Teresa/.
3. Adapted from Streiker, *An Encyclopedia of Humor*, 101.
4. Meg Meeker, *Strong Fathers, Strong Daughters* (New York: Ballantine, 2007), 51, italics mine.
5. Don Essig, *Motivational Minutes* (Lombard, IL: Successories Publishing, 1994), 29.

Chapter 7 Watch Out for Hazards

1. "Funny Steven Wright Quotes," Basic Funny Quotes, 2004, www.basicjokes.com/dquotes.php?aid=120.

Chapter 9 "Hello, My Name Is Dad"

1. Charles Barkley, *I May Be Wrong but I Doubt It* (New York: Random House, 2002), 215.
2. Streiker, *An Encyclopedia of Humor*, 127.
3. Gary Chapman, *The Five Love Languages of Teenagers* (Chicago: Northfield, 1997), 74.
4. Russert, *Wisdom of Our Fathers*, 24.

Chapter 10 Connect through Respect

1. Rodney Dangerfield, *I Don't Get No Respect* (Los Angeles: Price/Stern/Sloan, 1987).
2. If your kids are fighting with each other, it's because you don't have this book: Todd Cartmell, *Keep the Siblings, Lose the Rivalry* (Grand Rapids: Zondervan, 2003).
3. James Dobson, *Bringing Up Boys* (Carol Stream, IL: Tyndale, 2005), 68.

Chapter 11 Listen and Learn

1. Streiker, *An Encyclopedia of Humor*, 243.

Chapter 12 Connect as a Family

1. Stephen Covey, *The Seven Habits of Highly Effective Families* (New York: St. Martin's Griffin, 1997), 369.
2. You can find it at: http://www.geneva304.org/GHS/Athletics/Athletics.html.

Chapter 13 Be a Coach

1. "Will Rogers Quotes," Brainy Quote, 2010, http://www.brainyquote.com/quotes/authors/w/will_rogers_5.html.
2. Streiker, *An Encyclopedia of Humor*, 136.

Chapter 14 Save the Picnic

1. Chapman, *The Five Love Languages of Teenagers*, 141.

Chapter 15 Find the Horse

1. Streiker, *An Encyclopedia of Humor*, 122. In case you haven't noticed, this is a pretty good joke book.
2. Roger von Oech, *A Whack on the Side of the Head* (New York: Warner Books, 1990), 27–30, 75–76.
3. Christian Klemash, *How to Succeed in the Game of Life* (Kansas City, MO: Andrews McMeel Publishing, 2006), 55.

Chapter 17 Follow My Lead

1. Meeker, *Strong Fathers, Strong Daughters*, 151–52.

Chapter 19 Draw the Line

1. Victoria Rideout, Ulla Foehr, and Donald Roberts, *Generation M²: Media in the Lives of 8- to 18-Year-Olds* (Menlo Park, CA: Henry J. Kaiser Family Foundation, 2010), http://www.kff.org/entmedia/upload/8010.pdf.

Chapter 20 Wanted: Great Dads

1. John Eldredge, *You Have What It Takes* (Nashville: Thomas Nelson, 2004), 73–74.
2. Klemash, *How to Succeed in the Game of Life*, 194.
3. "Will Rogers Quotes," Brainy Quote, 2010, http://www.brainyquote.com/quotes/authors/w/will_rogers_2.html.

Todd Cartmell is a licensed clinical psychologist and a father of two. He is in full-time private practice in Wheaton, Illinois, where he works with children, adolescents, and families. He lives in Geneva, Illinois, with his family.

For more information about Todd Cartmell, parenting Q&A, practical articles, book excerpts, and workshop information, please visit www.drtodd.net.

Family expert
Rick Johnson
encourages and empowers fathers in their most important role.

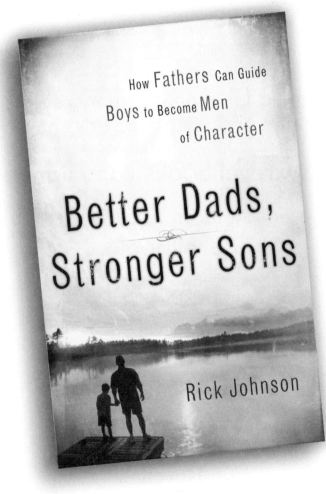

How Fathers Can Guide
Boys to Become Men
of Character

Better Dads, Stronger Sons

Rick Johnson

Revell
a division of Baker Publishing Group
www.RevellBooks.com

Available wherever books are sold.

Be the First
to Hear about
Other New Books
from Revell!

Sign up for announcements about
new and upcoming titles at

www.revellbooks.com/signup

Follow us on **twitter**
RevellBooks

Join us on **facebook**
Revell

Don't miss out on our great reads!

Revell
a division of Baker Publishing Group
www.RevellBooks.com